IN SUBJECTION

MERCER
UNIVERSITY PRESS

Endowed by
TOM WATSON BROWN
and
THE WATSON-BROWN FOUNDATION, INC.

IN SUBJECTION

Church Discipline in the

Early American South, 1760–1830

Jessica Madison

MERCER UNIVERSITY PRESS | MACON, GEORGIA

35 Years of Publishing Excellence

MUP/ H890

Published by Mercer University Press, Macon, Georgia 31207

1400 Coleman Avenue
Macon, Georgia 31207

9 8 7 6 5 4 3 2 1

Books published by Mercer University Press are printed on acid-free paper that meets the requirements of the American National Standard for Information Sciences—Permanence of Paper for Printed Library Materials.

Library of Congress Cataloging-in-Publication Data

Madison, Jessica, 1980-
In subjection : church discipline in the early American south, 1760-1830 / Jessica Madison. -- 1st [edition].
pages cm
Includes bibliographical references and index.
ISBN 978-0-88146-500-6 (hardback : alk. paper) -- ISBN 0-88146-500-3 (hardback : alk. paper)
1. Church discipline. 2. Baptists--Discipline--History--Sources.
3. Southern States--Church history. I. Title.
BR535.M33 2014
277.5'07--dc23

2014035253

CONTENTS

Acknowledgments / vi

List of Tables / vii

Preface / viii

1: Subjection: A Cultural Consensus 1

2: Unity and Discord / 32

3: Crucifying the Carnal Man / 58

4: Fellowlabourers / 91

5: Promiscuity and Marriage / 115

Conclusion: Meeting Adjourned / 149

Works Cited / 165

Index / 177

ACKNOWLEDGMENTS

I wish to thank the members of my dissertation committee: Director Dan Smith, the late Lance Banning, the late Dave Bowman, Ron Eller, Phil Harling, and Karl Raitz. Much of my research was made possible by the fine library staff at the University of Kentucky, Furman University, and Wake Forest University, and by a research travel grant from the UK Graduate School. I appreciate all the colleagues and friends who have read drafts and offered insight. I am also grateful to the church clerks who recorded these minute books and to all the archivists who have preserved the old church records for future generations. Special thanks to Mercer University Press for believing in this project and making the dream of publication become a reality. Finally, I wish to thank the members of Landmark Baptist Church in Annville, Kentucky, for their generous support and inspiration.

> "Unto him be glory in the church by Christ Jesus
> throughout all ages, world without end. Amen."
> Ephesians 3:21, KJV

List of Tables

Table 1.1	Membership Statistics	21
Table 2.1	Gossip Cases	44
Table 2.2	Language Cases	47
Table 2.3	Falsehood Cases	49
Table 2.4	Heresy Cases	54
Table 3.1	Census Statistics	69
Table 3.2	Skewarkey Taxpayers	71

PREFACE

According to the narrative commonly accepted by historians, Southern women of the eighteenth and early nineteenth centuries resented their own subordinate position, as well as that of slaves. In this version, marriage and slavery were twin institutions white men devised to maintain social control. In recent revisions to this story, elite women accepted their subordination as well as slavery as part of a package deal that served their self-interest.[1] There likely were women who fit into both categories, but what about the many non-elite women who appear to have accepted their prescribed role in Southern society? Could it be that churches, sometimes cast as a complicit villain in the oppression plot, actually won genuine submission by upholding a moral code that subjected both men and women to reciprocal standards of conduct?[2]

---

[1] Anne Firor Scott argued in 1970 that elite Southern women opposed the subjection of both themselves and slaves (*The Southern Lady: From Pedestal to Politics 1830–1930* [Chicago: University of Chicago Press, 1970]). For challenges to this view, see Elizabeth Fox-Genovese, *Within the Plantation Household: Black and White Women of the Old South* (Chapel Hill: University of North Carolina Press, 1988); Laura Edwards, *Gendered Strife and Confusion: The Political Culture of Reconstruction* (Chicago: University of Illinois Press, 1997); Drew Gilpin Faust, *Mothers of Invention: Women of the Slaveholding South in the American Civil War* (Chapel Hill: University of North Carolina Press, 1996); and Jane Turner Censer, *The Reconstruction of White Southern Womanhood 1865–1895* (Baton Rouge: Louisiana State University Press, 2003).

[2] According to some historians, a "great evangelical switch" occurred during this period, wherein evangelical leaders abandoned radical egalitarianism to join the rest of their society's leaders in supporting patriarchy. In order to win acceptance of Southern men, they adopted a new position concerning the rules of class, race, and gender. It seems more likely that an evangelical consensus about a God-ordained system of subjection appears to have remained considerably uniform across time, place, and denomination. Few evangelicals ever

Evidence for a double standard of moral behavior can certainly be found in the history of Southern society. For example, men could drink and duel without attracting negative attention. Men and women were assigned different roles in the church, but in matters of church discipline they were on equal footing.[3] Rather than simply empowering superiors over inferiors,

---

argued for complete equality, and few ever swung over to the other extreme. For examples of the "switch" assimilation theory, see Donald Mathews, *Religion in the Old South* (Chicago: University of Chicago Press, 1977); Robert Calhoon, *Evangelicals and Conservatives in the Early South, 1740–1861* (Columbia: University of South Carolina Press, 1988); Cynthia Lyerly, *Methodism and the Southern Mind,* 1770–1810 (New York: Oxford University Press, 1998); and Christine Heyrman, *Southern Cross: The Beginnings of the Bible Belt* (Chapel Hill: University of North Carolina Press, 1997). Whereas Rhys Isaac saw in evangelicalism a substantial challenge to patriarchal institutions, Heyrman argued that evangelicalism never gained significant influence until it had thrown its weight in support of patriarchy. Rhys Isaac, *The Transformation of Virginia, 1740–1790* (Chapel Hill: University of North Carolina Press, 1982). It was not, Heyrman argued, until evangelical Baptists, Methodists, and Presbyterians compromised their class, race, and gender egalitarianism to support patriarchy that they were able to establish a foothold in the South. She made a convincing argument that the evangelical "Bible Belt" was slow in forming, but it seems probable that the compromises leading to their growth were more religious than social (6). Her points on gender are especially shaky, resting on scattered anecdotes of a few Methodists and Separate Baptists. For works dealing more specifically with gender, see Stephanie McCurry, *Masters of Small Worlds: Yeoman Households, Gender Relations, and the Political Culture of the Antebellum South Carolina Low Country* (New York: Oxford University Press, 1995); Kathleen Brown, *Good Wives, Nasty Wenches and Anxious Patriarchs: Gender, Race and Power in Colonial Virginia* (Chapel Hill: University of North Carolina Press, 1996); and Susan Juster, *Disorderly Women: Sexual Politics and Evangelicalism in Revolutionary New England* (London: Cornell University Press, 1994).

[3] For more on the role of churches in either challenging or assimilating with Southern society, see also Jewel L. Spangler, *Virginians Reborn: Anglican Monopoly, Evangelical Dissent, and the Rise of the Baptists in the Late Eighteenth Century* (Charlottesville: University of Virginia Press, 2008); Scott Stephan, *Redeeming the Southern Family: Evangelical*

church discipline upheld a system of subjection with mutual obligations for all—men, women, parents, children, masters, and servants. As a result, many Southern women internalized the idea of subjection, regarding it not as bondage but as a system of relationships that served their interests well. When husbands were guilty of drunkenness, adultery, or violence, their wives could take the matter before the church. Even a slave woman, although involuntarily placed under a master's authority, could use church discipline to hold him accountable for abuse.

We can better understand this consensus by recognizing a distinction between "oppression" and "subjection." Oppression suggests an involuntary power relationship between superior and inferior. Subjection, on the other hand, suggests a voluntary submission in a relationship of mutual consent.

In exploring this culture of subjection, I hope to shed light on the rationale behind it, its nature, and its limits. What follows is not the story of gender conflict but of a misunderstood "moral economy" with expectations for all church members.[4] The definition of moral economy used here is broader than an economic term. Rather, it refers to a consensus regarding proper behavior in general, the reciprocal relationship church members were to

---

Women and Domestic Devotion in the Antebellum South (Athens: University of Georgia Press, 2011); Erskine Clarke, *Our Southern Zion: A History of Calvinism in the South Carolina Low Country, 1690–1990* (Tuscaloosa: University Alabama Press, 1996); and S. Scott Rohrer, *Hope's Promise: Religion and Acculturation in the Southern Backcountry* (Tuscaloosa: University Alabama Press, 2005).

[4] In describing the "moral economy" of English food riots, historian E. P. Thompson defined the term as a "popular consensus as to what were legitimate and what were illegitimate practices." E. P. Thompson, "The Moral Economy of the English Crowd in the Eighteenth Century," *Customs in Common: Studies in Traditional Popular Culture* (New York: The New Press, 1993). Rachel Klein used the term "Christian economy" to describe the organic vision of order evident in church records (*Unification of a Slave State: The Rise of the Planter Class in the South Carolina Backcountry, 1760–1808* [Chapel Hill: University of North Carolina Press, 1990] 298).

share in all walks of life. Men and women alike were to be in subjection to the expectations for their station. In the eyes of contemporaries, each link in the chain of subjection held the whole together and ultimately answered to God. These men and women all bowed their heads to that common Master.

What follows is an attempt to define this system of subjection more accurately, using North and South Carolina Baptist church record books as the primary source of evidence. Why Baptist record books? This neglected source of evidence is valuable because of the independent, congregational nature of grassroots church government. Not governed by distant presbyteries, independent Baptist congregations offer the best available window into what happened inside the walls of meetinghouses and reflect the views of a representative sample of laymen and women. Discipline cases are particularly insightful because they record a wide variety of proceedings against wayward members; Baptist churches did not allow their members to sue one another in civil courts. It is fortunate that churches kept detailed records of their business meetings, especially considering the scarcity of other types of documents. Sermons (from any denomination), for example, are scant for this period in the South. Although a few of the more prominent preachers wrote and published their sermons, most either delivered them extemporaneously or failed to preserve their notes for posterity.[5]

Baptist church record books also serve as a window into the world outside the meetinghouse walls. When compared with records from other denominations, Baptists differed little from other religious groups with respect to gender expectations. Comparing the records of the Baptist churches with secular records helps us understand the society as a whole. Patricia Bonomi claims that most members of Southern society were

---

[5] Some sermons delivered at Baptist association meetings have been recorded, but they tend to be theological in nature. Oliver Hart's sermon against dancing, as will be seen, is an exception.

regular churchgoers, and that the South's religious vitality has been underestimated. Bertram Wyatt-Brown, on the other hand, sees Southern society as a crude, heathen place where men were particularly uncivilized. Christine Heyrman's more moderate assessment that evangelical religion gradually mounted a challenge to the social status quo is likely more accurate. What churches taught concerning women's subjection presented no challenge to most Southerners, but to a greater extent than most, Baptist churches also demanded a form of subjection from men. While they shared their "world's" expectation that women be in subjection to men, they also critiqued the "worldly" behavior of wayward members, men included. Churches insisted that men and women both be subjected to a higher standard of conduct than society alone required.[6]

I have chosen to focus on thirty[7] Baptist churches from four regions of the Carolinas, the center of the early American South.[8]

---

[6] Patricia Bonomi, *Under the Cope of Heaven: Religion, Society, and Politics in Colonial America* (New York: Oxford University Press, 1986).

[7] John Asplund's 1790 *Register of the Baptist Denomination* reported approximately 100 Baptist churches in North Carolina and 70 in South Carolina; this study focuses on thirty of those 170 churches. John Asplund, *The Annual Register of the Baptist Denomination in North America* (1791; repr., Lafayette TN: Church History Research and Archives, 1979).

[8] *Bear Creek Baptist Church Records* (1787), Chatham County NC (North Carolina Baptist Historical Collection, Z. Smith Reynolds Library, Wake Forest University: Winston-Salem NC), 1801–1859; *Brier Creek Baptist Church Records* (1783), Ronda NC (North Carolina Baptist Historical Collection, Z. Smith Reynolds Library, Wake Forest University: Winston-Salem NC), 1783–1955; *Cashie Baptist Church Records* (1771), Windsor NC (North Carolina Baptist Historical Collection, Z. Smith Reynolds Library, Wake Forest University: Winston-Salem NC), 1791–1925; *Eaton's[-Dutchman's Creek] Baptist Church Records* (1772), Mocksville NC (North Carolina Baptist Historical Collection, Z. Smith Reynolds Library, Wake Forest University: Winston-Salem NC), 1772–1902; *Flat River [Primitive] Baptist Church Records* (1777), Person County NC (North Carolina Baptist Historical Collection, Z. Smith Reynolds Library, Wake Forest University: Winston-Salem NC), 1786–1945; *Jersey Baptist Church Records* (1758),

Davidson County NC (North Carolina Baptist Historical Collection, Z. Smith Reynolds Library, Wake Forest University: Winston-Salem NC), 1784–1797; *Lick Fork [Primitive] Baptist Church Records* (1786), Rockingham County NC (North Carolina Baptist Historical Collection, Z. Smith Reynolds Library, Wake Forest University: Winston-Salem NC), 1786–1921; *Poplar Spring[s] Baptist Church Records* (1788), Zebulon NC (North Carolina Baptist Historical Collection, Z. Smith Reynolds Library, Wake Forest University: Winston-Salem NC), 1788–1882; *Sandy Creek Baptist Church Records* (1770), Louisburg NC (North Carolina Baptist Historical Collection, Z. Smith Reynolds Library, Wake Forest University: Winston-Salem NC), 1771–1845; *Sandy Run Baptist Church Records* (1788), Cleveland County NC (North Carolina Baptist Historical Collection, Z. Smith Reynolds Library, Wake Forest University: Winston-Salem NC), 1782–1970; *Skewarkey [Primitive] Baptist Church Records* (1787), Martin County NC (North Carolina Baptist Historical Collection, Z. Smith Reynolds Library, Wake Forest University: Winston-Salem NC), 1786–1876; *South Fork of Roaring River Baptist Church Records* (1779), Wilkes County NC (original records copied by Mr. and Mrs. Stratton Hammon, Louisville KY, fmoran.com/ wilkes/roaring.html), 1785–1797; *Wheeleys [Primitive] Baptist Church Records* (1791), Bushy Fork NC (North Carolina Baptist Historical Collection, Z. Smith Reynolds Library, Wake Forest University: Winston-Salem NC), 1791; *Yadkin Baptist Church Records* (1779), Patterson NC (North Carolina Baptist Historical Collection, Z. Smith Reynolds Library, Wake Forest University: Winston-Salem NC), 1787–1839; *Ashley River Baptist Church Records* (1736), Charleston SC (South Carolina Baptist Historical Collection, James B. Duke Library, Furman University, Greenville SC), 1736–1769; *Black Creek Baptist Church Records* (1798), Darlington SC (South Carolina Baptist Historical Collection, James B. Duke Library, Furman University, Greenville SC), 1798–1896; *Boiling Springs Baptist Church Records* (1772), Spartanburg SC (South Carolina Baptist Historical Collection, James B. Duke Library, Furman University, Greenville SC), 1792–1822; *Brushy Creek Baptist Church Records* (1795), Greenville SC (South Carolina Baptist Historical Collection, James B. Duke Library, Furman University, Greenville SC), 1794–1827; *Bush River Baptist Church Records* (1771), Newberry SC (South Carolina Baptist Historical Collection, James B. Duke Library, Furman University, Greenville SC), 1791–1949; *Cashaway[-Mount Pleasant-Mechanicsville] Baptist Church Records* (1767), Darlington SC (South Carolina Baptist Historical Collection, James B. Duke Library, Furman University, Greenville SC), 1767–1867. Cashaway and Mount Pleasant

As shown on the map, the Coastal Plain lay to the east of the Fall Line, with the Piedmont and Blue Ridge Mountains to the west. This Fall Line, along with the present state boundary line, divides our area of study into the Low Country (eastern) and Up Country (western) regions of North and South Carolina. Few Baptist churches were established in the eastern regions of the Carolinas in the first half of the eighteenth century, and few appeared in the west prior to the end of the century.

Many sets of eighteenth-century church records have been lost. Of the record books that have survived from the eighteenth century, I have included as many as possible to ensure that the data is representative. Naturally, some sets are more comprehensive than others. While the majority of the records I

---

merged in 1791 and renamed the church Mechanicsville in 1818; *Cedar Spring[s] Baptist Church Records* (1786), Spartanburg SC (South Carolina Baptist Historical Collection, James B. Duke Library, Furman University, Greenville SC), 1794–1972; *Clear Springs Baptist Church Records* (1803), Greenville SC (South Carolina Baptist Historical Collection, James B. Duke Library, Furman University, Greenville SC), 1803–1953; *First Woodruff Baptist Church Records* (1787), Spartanburg County SC (Southern Baptist Historical Library and Archives, Southern Baptist Convention, Nashville TN), 1787–1804; *Gum Branch Baptist Church Records* (1796), Darlington SC (South Carolina Baptist Historical Collection, James B. Duke Library, Furman University, Greenville SC), 1796–1953; *Reedy River Baptist Church Records* (1788), Greenville SC (South Carolina Baptist Historical Collection, James B. Duke Library, Furman University, Greenville SC), 1799–1914; *Shoal Creek Baptist Church Records* (1795), Oconee SC (South Carolina Baptist Historical Collection, James B. Duke Library, Furman University, Greenville SC), 1796–1853; *Turkey Creek Baptist Church Records* (1785), Abbeville SC (South Carolina Baptist Historical Collection, James B. Duke Library, Furman University, Greenville SC), 1785–1909; *Tyger Baptist Church Records* (1793), Greenville SC (South Carolina Baptist Historical Collection, James B. Duke Library, Furman University, Greenville SC), 1801–1911; *Welsh Neck Baptist Church Records* (1738), Darlington SC (South Carolina Baptist Historical Collection, James B. Duke Library, Furman University, Greenville SC), 1737–1991. Hereafter, church records will be cited by the church name only.

studied were from 1760–1810, the entire range spanned 1730–1830. The study ends with the 1820s, a time when many churches were beginning to abandon church discipline and redefine the moral economy of subjection.

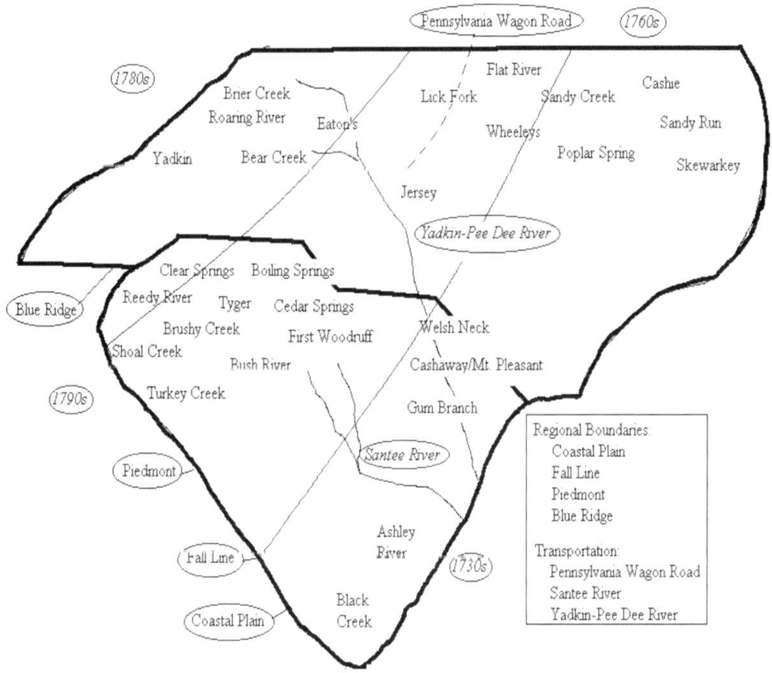

Low Country South Carolina was the home of the Charleston Baptist Association, the second Baptist association to be established in America (the first was in Philadelphia). During the 1730s Ashley River Baptist Church was established near Charleston, and the same decade Welsh Neck Baptist Church appeared along the Pee Dee River to the north. The church at Ashley River died out around the time of the American Revolution, but Welsh Neck Baptist Church continued and organized a church at Cashaway in the 1760s. Other churches continued to be organized in this region of South Carolina during the second half of the century. In 1765, churches in Low Country North Carolina formed the Kehukee Association and began correspondence with the Baptist Associations of Charleston and Philadelphia. Among them were Sandy Run Baptist Church in Bertie County and Sandy Creek Baptist Church in Granville County. In the 1780s and 90s, younger churches were also found among the Kehukee association's members. At the same time, churches were also beginning to spring up along the Yadkin River and in other parts of Up Country North Carolina, as well as along rivers in the Up Country section of South Carolina.[9]

The consensus regarding appropriate behavior (or moral economy) apparent in these church records appears to have been remarkably uniform across time and space. The chapters that

---

[9] The Charleston record book has been lost. See Oliver Hart Diary, 1741–1780 (Oliver Hart Papers, South Caroliniana Library, Columbia SC). For more on the history of these churches and their associations see David Benedict, *A General History of the Baptist Denomination in America*, vol. 2 (Boston: Lincoln & Edmands, 1813); Leah Townsend, *South Carolina Baptists, 1670–1805* (1935; repr., Baltimore: Genealogical Publishing Co., 1974); George Washington Paschal, *History of North Carolina Baptists*, vol. 1 (Raleigh NC: Edwards & Broughton Co., 1930); C. B. Hassell and S. Hassell, *History of the Church of God* (1886; repr., Ellenwood GA: Old School Hymnal Co., 1983); Wood Furman, *A History of the Charleston Association of Baptist Churches in the State of South-Carolina* (Charleston: J. Hoff, 1811); Lemuel Burkitt and Jesse Read, *A concise history of the Kehukee Baptist Association from its original rise to the present time* (Halifax NC: A. Hodge, 1803).

follow explore patterns found in discipline cases that demonstrate the expectations of that moral economy for both men and women, and how churches attempted to regulate it. Chapter 1, "Subjection: A Cultural Consensus," introduces the concept of a socio-religious consensus concerning a system of subjection that encompassed men and women, masters and servants, parents and children, authorities and subjects. The biblical foundation for this system will be explored, as well as the way in which it was manifested in church business. Chapter 2, "Unity and Discord," examines cases of general contention between church members, demonstrating that churches expected brothers and sisters to submit to each other in Christian fellowship. Men and women were assigned distinct roles, but they were dealt with for breaking the bonds of unity without significant respect to gender. Chapter 3, "Crucifying the Carnal Man," focuses on discipline cases wherein men were brought under subjection to church standards. Charges of intoxication, violence, vulgarity, and carnality were usually directed at male members, and occasionally their accusers were female. Chapter 4, "Fellowlabourers," examines financial matters, demonstrating that while expectations varied for men and women, they both bore financial responsebilities as church members, and both were held equally accounttable for their secular dealings. Chapter 5, "Promiscuity and Marriage," concentrates on the relationships between husbands and wives, a common symbol of Christian subjection. Discipline cases for fornication, marital disputes, and adultery punished men and women with surprisingly equal rigor, even while reinforcing an institution that prescribed them different positions.

In the end, a much clearer view emerges of this culture of subjection, believed by its advocates to be ordered by God for the good of all. This system did not target one group as much as it fit all together with mutual privileges and obligations. A woman's many obligations were balanced by a man's duties of fidelity, sobriety, provision, and protection. Relationships between these men and women were not always rosy, to be sure. Men often failed to live up to the standards they were expected to follow. Individual women sometimes challenged the "divine order of the sexes," but as a group they rarely did. Was this due to their ignorance, lack of opportunity, or genuine contentment? Instead of placing ourselves in their shoes and imagining what they *must* have thought and felt, let us listen to their "voices" whisper (and sometimes shout) through the pages of these church record books. Recent historical works on this subject paint a dark—and possibly distorted—picture of this "moral economy" by interpreting it as oppressive, when in fact church discipline empowered the oppressed with a voice. Church records reveal a historical drama that is cast with round characters who are neither saintly heroes nor intriguing villains and colored by the real life combination of conflict and consensus. Such a story can be just as exciting as any other grand narrative, and it is certainly much more believable.

1

SUBJECTION
A CULTURAL CONSENSUS

Eighteenth-century Southerners believed in a system of proper spheres for everyone. Society was to be ordered in many ways. Civil and religious authorities, masters and slaves, husbands and wives, parents and children, all had their place in a chain ultimately subject to God. Modern sociologists call it "patriarchy"; contemporaries would have called it "good order." No doubt some who stood higher in the ranks, particularly plantation owners, had reasons of self-interest to support such an order, but to understand such a general consensus only in terms of self-interest is anachronistic. The subject cannot be properly understood without recognizing the role of religion in convincing even the lowest of subjects that this order was just and beneficial. This chapter will first examine the way in which Scripture influenced Baptist churches' culture of subjection. Southerners were quick to cite Scripture as their standard of faith and practice. Although they did not always act consistently with it, the historical evidence found in Baptist church covenants and discipline cases shows that Scripture did much to influence their actions. Second, this chapter will consider a variety of Baptist religious leaders who, despite their many other differences, shared a mutual defense of subjection. Third, it will be argued that the culture of woman's subjection went beyond its religious roots and permeated society, mutually reinforced both by churches of all denominations and the norms of their unchurched neighbors. Society as a whole understood the common language of subjection. The subjection of women was a part of the shared culture; churches' more controversial insistence on man's subjection will be discussed in a later chapter. Finally, I will describe how conceptions of subjection were manifested in the roles of men and women in church business. While there were certainly boundaries for women in Baptist churches, those boundaries were not as confining as one might expect.

Baptists appeared throughout the South in increasing numbers following the First Great Awakening, which gained momentum in the South in the second half of the eighteenth century. These Baptists were known for the autonomous polity of independent congregations. Their theology, along with that of other evangelical groups, emphasized the new birth that was necessary for salvation. The baptism of believers was a symbol that the former man had been buried and raised to walk in newness of life. Saints were to be new creatures, separate from the sinful, carnal world of unregenerate men. By the Second Great Awakening in the nineteenth century, Baptists were no longer a minority group of Southerners. They did remain a minority, however, in mindset. Even when Baptists came to rank among the most influential religious groups in the South, they continued to stress their status as outsiders to the world. The evangelical doctrine of the new birth influenced the practice of church discipline in making sure that professing believers acted the part.

Methodist Bishop John Early, when he toured North Carolina in 1808, noted in his journal that he preached on the subject of the various commissions given to civil and religious leaders, husbands and wives, and masters and servants. Early commented that "Some were displeased and some delighted but none of these things moved me."[1] What might have displeased and delighted various members of his audience? Without a written record of that sermon's contents, it is impossible to know exactly what Early preached on the subject. We do, however, know that he used Scripture as an authority. Assuming he interpreted well-known passages much as his contemporaries did, we can make an educated guess concerning his message. In such a sermon, a Southern preacher of his time likely would have included biblical texts instructing citizens to honor and obey civil authorities in the secular world. He would have directed his audience to passages commanding servants to honor and obey their masters, even difficult ones, and to passages commanding masters to treat their servants justly. He would then have demanded subjection of churches as well, reminding members to honor pastors and to submit themselves to one another as brothers and sisters in Christ. Early likely applied the doctrine of subjection to homes as well, reminding children to obey their parents and fathers not to provoke their children. A sermon discussing the relationship between husbands and wives would almost certainly have echoed the biblical instructions for wives to *submit* unto husbands, and husbands to *love* their wives. Instructions for husbands and wives were different but not one-sided. According to the Bible, husbands and wives both *owned* one another's bodies and *owed* each other "due benevolence."[2]

---

[1] John Early Diary, 1807–1814, Southern Historical Collection (Louis Round Wilson Special Collections Library, University of North Carolina, Chapel Hill NC).

[2] For the biblical foundation for the doctrine of subjection by citizens to civil authorities, see 1 Pet 2:13-17; Rom 13:1-7. For servants and masters, see Titus 2:9-10; 1 Pet 2:18; 1 Tim 6:1-2; Eph 6:5-9; Col 3:22-4:1. For Christian fellowship, see 1 Pet 5:1-5; Heb 13:7, 17; Titus 2:1-7; Eph 5:21; 1 Tim 5:1-2, 17; Phil 2:1-11; 1 Pet 2:21. For children and

Baptist preachers likely delivered sermons throughout Southern churches on the same subject Early chose on that occasion. Few sermons by Baptist preachers survive from this period, but church covenants and records of church business meetings show that scriptural guidelines did much to shape the practice of Baptist churches with regard to subjection. If actions speak louder than words, then church record books are a better source of information than a collection of sermons would be on what churches actually practiced.

In the Tyger Baptist Church Confession of Faith, church members promised to "Submit to Civil Government." Scattered evidence suggests that Baptists of the Carolinas were considered law-abiding citizens from the beginning of settlement. When South Carolina offered incentives to settlers in the backcountry of the 1730s, the government welcomed Welsh Baptists from Pennsylvania as a reliable buffer to protect the Low Country against slave insurrections and Indian attacks. The records of Baptist churches in the middle colonies, from which many of the first churches in the South traced their roots, reflect loyalty to the English crown prior to the American Revolution. In fact, several records indicate reluctance to change their position hastily, even in the early days of the Revolution.[3]

One of the earliest episodes of church-state relations in the South was the Regulator Movement in western North Carolina. The Regulators (especially strong in Orange, Anson, and Rowan counties) had a number of grievances against Governor Tryon's administration. High taxes, corrupt administration, and limited benefits, combined with disregard for their protests, led the

---

parents, see Exod 20:12; Eph 6:1-4; Col 3:20-21. For husbands and wives, see Eph 5:22-33; Col 3:18-19; 1 Pet 3:1-7; 1 Cor 7:3-5.

[3] Jessica Flinchum [Madison], "Reluctant Revolutionaries: The Philadelphia Baptist Association and the American Revolution," *Pennsylvania History* 74/2 (Spring 2007): 173–93.

Regulators to take up arms against the colonial government at the Battle of Alamance in 1771.[4] Governor Tryon described the Regulators as "a faction of Quakers and Baptists," but when Baptist historian Morgan Edwards investigated the matter the following year, he concluded that "there were but 7 of the denomination of Baptists; and these were expelled by the societies they belonged unto," in accordance with the Sandy Creek Baptist Association's resolution of 1769 that "If any of our members shall take up arms against the legal authority, or aid and abet them that do so, he shall be excommunicated."[5]

The commandment to obey civil authorities was interpreted differently by various Baptist churches in the context of the American Revolution. Many Baptists were willing to rebel against King and Parliament and to transfer their loyalties to new state governments. Others, however, could not do so in good conscience. William Cook, pastor of Eaton Baptist Church, was among them. In 1775, Cook signed "The Protest," a Tory document denouncing the patriots, for which he was brought before the Rowan County Committee of Safety for examination. This scrutiny appears to have silenced Cook, but whether his views changed is uncertain. That same year, his church resolved

---

[4] See Marvin Michael Kay, "The North Carolina Regulation, 1766–1776: A Class Conflict" in Alfred Young, ed., *The American Revolution: Explorations in the History of American Radicalism* (DeKalb: Northern Illinois University Press, 1976) and Marjoleine Kars, *Breaking Loose Together: The Regulator Rebellion in Pre-Revolutionary North Carolina* (Chapel Hill: University of North Carolina Press, 2002).

[5] David Benedict, *A General History of the Baptist Denomination in America*, vol. 2 (Boston: Lincoln & Edmands, 1813) 116. Paschal disagrees about the sympathies of Baptists, interpreting a friendly letter from the Kehukee Association to Governor Martin as evidence of their support for the Regulators (George Washington Paschal, *History of North Carolina Baptists*, vol. 1 [Raleigh NC: Edwards & Broughton Co., 1930] 425).

that members should be at liberty to join the American cause or to abstain; either way they should be treated with love. In 1777, the church pledged its allegiance to state laws, and the following year it excommunicated members who had signed the Protest.[6] Thomas Norris, pastor of Bush River Baptist Church during the Revolution, was also known as a Tory for teaching non-resistance. He was imprisoned and several times refused to silence his message as a condition of his release.[7] Evan Pugh of Cashaway Baptist Church was also caught in the middle of the conflict.[8] Most Baptist preachers, however, such as Oliver Hart, are remembered as patriots. Baptists of the American South sometimes disagreed over which authorities to recognize, but they shared the conviction that it was their duty to submit to legitimate authority, whether that was England or the new United States.

Biblical instructions to servants and masters were less divisive. Church covenants provide evidence that Southern churches echoed such instructions, and discipline cases for transgressions against these instructions to masters and servants confirmed that churches sought to enforce compliance. Mechanicsville Baptist Church stated in Article 11 of its Covenant,

> While we would be taught by the wisest of men not to raise our servants in delicacy and indolence and would recollect that obedience is due from them to us, we feel bound to avoid acts of cruelty towards them—point out to them the course of duty—open the way for them to receive instruction from a preached gospel, and supply them with food and raiment

[6] Paschal, *History of North Carolina Baptists*, 470–71.

[7] "History of Bush River Baptist Church," collected with church records, citing John B. O'Neall and John A. Chapman, *The Annals of Newberry County, in two parts* (Newberry SC: Aull & Houseal, 1892).

[8] See introduction to Horace Fraser Rudisill, *The Diaries of Evan Pugh, 1762–1801* (Florence SC: St. David's Society, 1993).

becoming their station and worthy of the Christian character which we sustain.

Turkey Creek Baptist Church excommunicated a woman in 1799 who "imperiously abus'd her servant," in addition to being "a contentious person in her family." The authority of masters over their slaves was not absolute, as evidenced by disciplinary action in cases of excessive physical punishment. Furthermore, slaves were occasionally seen testifying in discipline cases involving their masters.[9]

In the context of the Bible, the master/servant relationship differed from American slavery. Hebrew servitude usually involved people of similar ethnicity, resulted from indebtedness or warfare, and was temporary, similar to the indentured servitude of eighteenth-century America, which was race-based and binding for generations. In fact, the chapter following the famous Ten Commandments in Exodus condemns the type of kidnapping that fueled the Atlantic slave trade. Nevertheless, many eagerly misapplied Scripture supporting servitude to their own brand of slavery, reminding their black "servants" that the Apostle Paul instructed the runaway Philemon to return to his master where he belonged.[10]

Church covenants also echoed scriptural instructions with regard to subjection in churches and families. Covenants repeatedly stated members' promise to give themselves up to one another and to walk together in brotherly love. Several discipline cases illustrated churches' views of parental authority. Reedy River Baptist Church, for example, ordered a father in 1814 to "reprove his son sharply." Turkey Creek Baptist Church

[9] For example, Tyger heard testimony from slaves when a white man was charged with "uncleanness" in 1805.

[10] Exod 21:16; Philemon. See also Mitchell Snay, *Gospel of Disunion: Religion and Separatism in the Antebellum South* (New York: Cambridge University Press, 1993).

affirmed by queries in 1801 and again in 1806 that mothers as well as fathers had authority over their children. The authority to discipline children, however, was not absolute; the same church examined a mother in 1802 for the charge of "whipping one of her children unreasonable." Church discipline cases involving couple disputes show that churches required mutual respect of husbands and wives. Husbands and wives who were contentious or abusive were both subject to the censure of the church. Further evidence of the practical application of subjection doctrine in churches can also be found in the silence of women in church assemblies. As will be seen, this silence was not total in eighteenth-century Baptist churches. There were certain times when women were permitted to speak, but in general their voices were muted. They were not to speak, much less teach men, in religious meetings.[11]

At one level, wives were in subjection to husbands, just as children were to parents and servants to masters. At a different level, all church members were united as one body in their subjection to each other and to God. As will be seen in the historical evidence churches left behind, their moral economy was patterned after this scriptural ideal. The way the subjection of women was part of a larger system of subjection is clearly demonstrated by considering three verses together. First Peter

---

[11] Another symbol of women's subjection is the veil. Because God was the head of Christ, Christ the head of man, and man the head of woman, and distinct positions in this chain of "headship" were signified by headwear, men left their heads uncovered and women covered theirs when worshiping together. In the absence of references to challenges to this practice in the church records, it is likely that Southern churches did not depart from the centuries-old tradition of churches in Europe and other parts of the United States. For biblical teachings on headship and the silence of women, see 1 Cor 11:3-16; 14:33-35; 1 Tim 2:9-15.

admonishes, "wives, be in subjection to your own husbands" (3:1) Two chapters later, it commands church members, "all of you be subject one to another" (1 Pet 5:5). And finally, as stated in Ephesians, "the church is subject unto Christ" (5:24).

The Baptists of the eighteenth-century South were in many ways different from other religious groups of the day, and in some ways were even divided among themselves. Baptists to the east of the Fall Line were typically those of the "Regular" or "Particular" sort, so named for their belief in the Calvinistic doctrine of "particular redemption" (Christ died for only those predestined for salvation) as opposed to the "universal atonement" (Christ died for all) doctrine of many Separate Baptists. Those who populated the western ends of North and South Carolina were most often "Separate" Baptists, former New England Congregationalists who had become Baptists after the first Great Awakening and migrated in large numbers to the southern frontier in the 1750s and 60s. These formed the Sandy Creek Baptist Association in the 1750s. At first the Separates appeared too Arminian to the Regulars, but Separate and Regular Baptists came to agree more closely in doctrine after compromising on the doctrine of limited atonement.

Even with the disappearance of earlier divisions, the experiences of Up Country Baptists remained different in some ways from that of their Low Country brethren. On the fringe of settlement, they encountered waves of westward migration, early conflict with Native Americans, and later troubles between their own colonial government and the Regulators. But perhaps the most prominent feature of Up Country Baptist life was the revival phenomenon that began around 1800. Beginning among Presbyterians and Methodists, these revivals (for good or ill) could not be ignored by Baptists. Baptist ministers and church members sometimes participated in the massive inter-denominational camp meetings, but seldom did they partake in their communion services. More commonly, Baptists began to host their own camp meetings, which, according to their own accounts, were of more orderly demeanor and doctrine than those of Presbyterians and Methodists.[12]

Nevertheless, the extent of regional differences among Baptists throughout the South in this period should not be overemphasized. Neither should it be taken for granted that they were isolated from other American regions. Southern Regulars and Separates maintained communication with Baptists in the Middle Colonies, New England, and even the Old World from their earliest days. The Charleston Baptist Association, for example, immediately began correspondence with the Philadelphia Baptist Association upon its organization. For all their differences, Baptists shared some common convictions. As will be seen, some convictions cut across denominational lines as well. One of those convictions was a belief in the divine order of the sexes.

In the eighteenth century, belief in predestination and election was found not only among Baptists in the South, but also among some Presbyterians, Congregationalists, Anglicans, and even Methodists throughout North America and Europe. More divisive at the time was the Baptist doctrine of church polity. They were the ultimate "separatists." Unlike Protestant denominations who shared a common heritage of splitting from the Roman Catholic Church (either directly as in the case of Anglicans or indirectly as in the case of Puritans), many eighteenth-century Baptists denied any historical connection with Catholicism. They instead insisted that they originated with the constitution of the original "true church" during Christ's earthly ministry. Because of this special heritage, they viewed all other churches as Protestant daughters of "the great whore"

---

[12] See Benedict, *A General History of the Baptist Denomination in America*, 2:108, 164.

Catholicism, and condemned the "fornication" of mixing true religion with the false.[13] For this reason, they refused to recognize the authority of other churches to administer the ordinance and insisted on "re-baptizing" those who converted from Catholicism or Protestantism to the Baptist faith. Hence the name "Ana-baptist," which was later shortened to "Baptist." In the American South, the Anglican Church was established by law during the colonial period. Although dissenters experienced less persecution in the Carolinas than in Virginia, they still faced discriminatory policies such as taxation to support the established church.[14]

Although such doctrinal differences set these denominations apart, the doctrine of subjection cut across the divisions. For a prominent example of a Presbyterian authority of late seventeenth and early eighteenth-century England, consider Matthew Henry, author of *Matthew Henry's Commentary on the Whole Bible*. From his commentary, it is clear that neither he nor the majority of his readers had any reservation about a divine order of the sexes. In his exposition of Ephesians 5:21-33, the passage instructing wives to submit to their husbands "as unto the Lord," and husbands to love their wives, "even as Christ also loved the church," Henry asserted that the passage meant exactly what it seemed to say. In his words, "Whatever there is of uneasiness in this, it is an effect of sin coming into the world." He continues,

[13] J. M. Carroll, *The Trail of Blood* (Lexington: Ashland Avenue Baptist Church, 1931).

[14] For a discussion of discrimination faced by dissenters in the South, see Robert Semple and George W. Beale, *A History of the Rise and Progress of the Baptists in Virginia* (Richmond: Pitt and Dickinson, 1894) and Rhys Isaac, *The Transformation of Virginia, 1740–1790* (Chapel Hill: University of North Carolina Press, 1982).

> neither has reason to complain of the divine injunctions. The love which God requires from the husband in behalf of his wife will make amends for the subjection which he demands from her to her husband; and the prescribed subjection of the wife will be an abundant return for that love of the husband which God has made her due.[15]

Henry Pattillo, a Presbyterian of Granville County, North Carolina, offered similar advice to American husbands, wives, children, and servants in *The Plain Planter's Family Assistant*.[16] Pattillo combined religious and social reasons for Americans to attend to their proper roles. He reminded American men that the blessings God had bestowed upon them came with great responsibilities. Then, after exhorting heads of families to observe personal piety, he questioned them concerning their regard for their wives. He went on to suggest that American wives deserve special honor for their sacrifices in the late Revolution, and then challenged them to make certain their hearts and lives reflected becoming virtues such as trustworthiness, helpfulness, and meekness, in contrast to the "daughters of fury." Pattillo then credited women for their restraining influence on the vice of their husbands and challenged them to examine their spiritual state.

The Church of England and dissenters found much to disagree about in England and its colonies, but the subjection of women was not one of them. Richard Allestree, author of *The Whole Duty of Man*, also published *The Ladies Calling*. As the work's table of contents suggests, he encouraged women to

---

[15] Matthew Henry, *Matthew Henry's Commentary on the Whole Bible* (Grand Rapids: Zondervan Publishing House, 1978) Eph 5:21–33.

[16] Henry Pattillo, *The Plain Planter's Family Assistant* (Wilmington DE: James Adams, 1787). See Daniel Blake Smith, *Inside the Great House: Planter Family Life in Eighteenth-Century Chesapeake Society* (Ithaca: Cornell University Press, 1980).

cultivate modesty, meekness, compassion, affability, and piety in all walks of life. Part II, Section 2, "Of Wives," offers more specific exhortations to married women, dividing a wife's duty toward her husband into those to his person, his reputation, and his fortune. According to Allestree,

> The first debt to his Person is Love, which we find set as the prime Article in the marriage vow; and indeed that is the most essential requisite; without this 'tis only a Bargain and Compact, a Tyranny perhaps on the mans part, and a Slavery on the womans.... This it is which facilitates all other duties of marriage; makes the yoke fit so lightly, that it rather pleases then galls.

In addition to love, Allestree also emphasizes wifely obedience and criticizes those wives whose rebellion brings about their own destruction. He observes, "the imperiousness of a woman does often raise those storms, wherein her self is Shipwrack'd. How pleasantly might many women have lived if they had not affection dominion. Nay how much of their will might they have had, if they had not strugled for it."[17] According to Allestree, subjection was to a wife's advantage and insubordination was as much a disservice to herself as to her husband.

---

[17] Richard Allestree, "Of Wives," in *The Ladies Calling*, part 2, section 2 (Oxford: At the Theater in Oxford, 1673) 14. Allestree continues, "For let a man be of never so gentle a temper (unless his head be softer then his heart) such an usurpation will awake him to assert his right. But if he be of a sowr severe nature, if he have as great a desire of rule as she, backt with a much better title, what Tempests, what Hurricanes must two such opposite winds produce? And at last 'tis commonly the wives lot, after an uncreditable unjust war, to make as disadvantageous a peace; this (like all other ineffective rebellions) serving to straiten her yoke, to turn an ingenuous subjection into a slavish servitude: so that certainly it is not only vertue, but the wisdom of wives to do that upon duty, which at last they must (with more unsupportable circumstances) do upon necessity."

Even New England Congregationalists found common ground with such an ideology. In *A Well-Ordered Family*, Harvard President Benjamin Wadsworth wrote, "The husband's government ought to be gentle and easy, and the wife's obedience ready and cheerful."[18] A wife was to be under her husband's government, "Yet his government should not be with rigor, haughtiness, harshness, severity, but with the greatest love, gentleness, kindness, tenderness that may be. Though he governs her, he must not treat her as a servant, but as his own flesh; he must love her as himself." He charged husbands to treat their wives "lovingly and kindly," and wives to treat their husbands "lovingly and obediently." Religious authorities of the time, whether in England, New England, or the South, overwhelmingly shared a belief that men and women were to be in subjection, each in their respective way. In spite of all their doctrinal differences, such diverse groups as Baptists, Anglicans, Presbyterians, and Congregationalists could all say "amen" to this message.

According to some historians, Methodists did not share in this consensus, at least not in the early years of Methodism. This group has been considered the most reliable champion of egalitarian ideas concerning gender roles among early evangelicals. It is true that Methodists displayed a relatively liberal attitude toward the participation of women in religious affairs. Nevertheless, not even the Methodists substantiate the case for early egalitarianism without considerable limitations. Christine Heyrman admits that examples are limited to relating conversion experiences and offering extemporaneous prayers. Although a few early Methodists argued that women should be allowed to preach, they were in the minority. In spite of a few

---

[18] Benjamin Wadsworth, *A Well-Ordered Family* (Boston: B. Green, 1712).

advocates, "From their first appearance in the South, most Methodists as well as Baptists stopped short of endorsing preaching by women or any age or race...there is no evidence that Southern women, Methodist or Baptist, preached in their own neighborhoods or abroad." Heyrman points to the journals of a few Methodist (and one Baptist) ministers for evidence that, in some circles, women were permitted to speak in public religious gatherings.[19] But it is important to keep in mind that, even among the more egalitarian Methodists, much of the female voice was heard only in limited circumstances, such as testifying of conversion before a church meeting or praying and exhorting at religious "society" gathering in private homes.

To an even greater extent than Methodists, Separate Baptists also fail to provide substantial evidence of early gender egalitarianism. They did hold to some practices that Regular Baptists found peculiar. In addition to baptism and the Lord's Supper, they also observed rites such as love feasts, laying on of hands, foot washing, anointing the sick with oil, offering the right hand of fellowship, the kiss of charity, and devoting children. As Baptist historian David Benedict observed, "They also held to ruling elders, eldresses, deaconesses, and weekly communion." Some of those peculiarities, including eldresses and deaconesses, had already "fallen into disuse" by the time Benedict published his work in 1813.[20] But what exactly were the peculiarities? Morgan Edwards, perhaps the most prominent American Baptist preacher and historian prior to the Revolution, visited churches across the colonies to collect information

[19] These were Thomas Rankin, Jeremiah Norman, Francis Asbury, Joseph Travis, Henry Smith, and John (the Baptist) Taylor, Christine Heyrman, *Southern Cross: The Beginnings of the Bible Belt* (Chapel Hill: University of North Carolina Press, 1997) 166–67.

[20] Benedict, *A General History of the Baptist Denomination in America,* 2:107.

toward a history of the Baptists in America. In his 1768 *Customs of the Primitive Churches*, he observed that "The office of eldresses...consists in praying and teaching at their separate assemblies; presiding there for maintenance of rules and government; consulting with the sisters about matters of the Church which concern them, and representing their sense thereof to the attending at the unction of sick sisters; and at the baptism of women all may be done orderly."[21] In short, although differences did exist between and within denominations, there was very little doctrinal disagreement in the matter of gender roles. Such doctrinal statements by church authorities, of course, offer a limited understanding of practical application. Baptist church record books, however, offer a rare glimpse of daily practice. Members frequently transgressed the laws of subjection, but churches demanded satisfaction for such transgressions with significant consistency.

It is also clear that this consensus concerning women's subjection not only cut across denominational boundaries; it permeated Southern society as a whole. Although unchurched Southerners tended to be more lenient with men, there is little evidence that anyone challenged women's subjection. Whether or not they were concerned with subjection's biblical mandate, Southerners recognized the value of women's subjection in terms of preserving the status quo. Just as the institution of marriage seemed only natural and beneficial to society, a woman's subjection to her husband inside a marriage, and to her father outside of it, was almost taken for granted, as much so as differences in appearance between the sexes.

Caution should be taken, however, in assuming that this subjection was total, approaching oppression, in either religion

---

[21] Morgan Edwards, *The Customs of Primitive Churches*, vol. 8 (Philadelphia: Andrew Steuart, 1768).

or society. Cynthia Kierner has argued persuasively that the public/private "separate spheres" paradigm is too rigid to accurately fit society in Virginia and the Carolinas during the Colonial, Revolutionary, and Early Republican periods. Women routinely participated in public life without transgressing the bounds of feminine propriety by challenging men for public dominance.[22] Just as women found ways to participate in politics without taking up arms during the Revolution or voting for their representatives, women also could be active participants in church business without standing in the pulpit or serving as deacon. The evidence found in this sample of church records suggests that the subjection of women in the eighteenth- and early nineteenth-century Southern churches was much more moderate than is often supposed. The impartiality seen in the administration of church discipline suggests the need to distinguish between the existence of subjection, which is indisputable, and an abusive double standard, of which there is little evidence.

Baptist churches zealously followed their instructions to "purge out" members guilty of serious offenses, "not to keep company" with them, "with such an one no not to eat" when observing the Lord's Supper, to "judge them that are within," and to "put away" such persons from their number. The Bible forbade the practice of church members suing one another at civil law. Instead, churches were to judge disputes between members for themselves.[23] Tyger's Rules of Discipline ordered,

---

[22] Kierner writes, "White Southern women consistently participated in public life." She recognizes "the difficulties in distinguishing public from private and the extent to which these seemingly opposite spheres may have been overlapping or even interdependent" (*Beyond the Household: Women's Place in the Early South, 1700–1835* [London: Cornell University Press, 1998] 3).

[23] 1 Cor 5–6.

"Church members may not Law one with another."[24] The Kehukee Association in eastern North Carolina took the same position in response to a 1782 query: "Has a church any right to try causes of a civil nature? Answer: We look upon it a duty to be continued in the church."[25] For these reasons, discipline cases in these church record books are a fruitful source of information concerning the way offending members, men and women, were dealt with.

Baptist churches usually met monthly on a Saturday for business meetings, at which they would receive and dismiss members, and often put members on trial for offenses.[26] The discipline rate varied between churches. That of Low Country South Carolina was generally lower than average with approximately one discipline case per year. In other regions of the Carolinas, the norm was a few cases per year. A few zealous churches (such as Tyger) sometimes disciplined several members each month.

Most of these churches made a distinction between "suspension" and "excommunication" in disciplining members. Suspension was a state of probation during which a member was denied the usual privileges of voting and observing the Lord's Supper with the rest of the church. Suspended members were eventually either restored to full fellowship or excommunicated from the church, depending upon whether the church was

---

[24] For more examples of churches forbidding lawsuits among members, see Poplar Spring Baptist Church 1794, Welsh Neck Baptist Church 1787, and Skewarkey Baptist Church 1790/91, 1806.

[25] C. B. Hassell and S. Hassell, *History of the Church of God* (1886; repr., Ellenwood GA: Old School Hymnal Co., 1983) 830.

[26] See Greg Wills, *Democratic Religion: Freedom, Authority, and Church Discipline in the Baptist South, 1785–1900* (New York: Oxford University Press, 1997) 20–25 for a detailed discussion of procedure at business meetings.

satisfied with evidence of repentance.[27] The practice of suspension in churches is of uncertain origin. It does not appear to have been exercised in the first centuries of church history, but was quite common in eighteenth-century America. It may have developed as a result of logistic circumstances; in scattered frontier settlements, churches were not able to meet frequently. Theoretically, a church could find itself confronted with members in need of discipline each time it met. If a church obeyed biblical instructions to refrain from the Lord's Supper until such problems were resolved, and also to be patient and charitable in dealing with wayward members, the church might necessarily go for an extended period of time without opportunity to observe the ordinance. Some churches may have turned to the practice of suspension as a result of such circumstances. Its adoption, however, was not universal.

Poplar Spring Baptist Church considered the propriety of suspension in 1795 and concluded that it was without scriptural foundation and should not be practiced. The Kehukee Association concurred in a query of 1782.[28] Whether or not a church practiced suspension, offending members were usually given time to give the church satisfaction before being excommunicated. Other members were often sent as "messengers" to speak with them. The most common offense was non-attendance. Sometimes a church would send a delinquent a letter, in place of

---

[27] Janet Moore Lindman says the terms were "exclusion" and "excommunication" in Virginia (*A World of Baptists: Gender, Race, and Religious Community in Pennsylvania and Virginia, 1689–1825* [Minneapolis: University of Minnesota, 1994] 226). The Charleston Association Discipline distinguishes between "rebuke," "suspension," and "excommunication" (Charleston Baptist Association, *Summary of Church Discipline* [Charleston: CBA, 1783] ch. 1).

[28] C. B. Hassell and S. Hassell, *History of the Church of God* (1886; repr., Ellenwood GA: Old School Hymnal Co., 1983) 830.

a personal messenger, admonishing them to their "duty." The length of time a church would "bear with" a disorderly member varied depending on the church and the nature of the offense.[29]

Baptist churches clearly made distinctions between male and female members. This is immediately evident upon examining surviving membership lists included in some record books. Membership lists often divided men and women into separate columns or pages, and some also listed white and black members separately. These lists also tell us that churches varied in size between dozens and hundreds of members. As the chart below reveals, male and female membership was generally equal throughout most of the eighteenth century, and early records listed most members as couples. In a region's early years of settlement, migration patterns often revolved around family units. Once settled in a new home, individuals had greater opportunity to join a nearby congregation independently of a family group.

[29] Suspension may have originated with the inconvenience of meeting monthly due to geographical dispersion; perhaps members found it difficult to observe the Lord's Supper when each meeting was burdened by new discipline cases. Jean Friedman cites sources for Presbyterian and Methodist church discipline procedure: "In the Baptist and Methodist churches male elders presented the case to the congregation, while in the Presbyterian church the accused appeared before a board of elders…." (*The Enclosed Garden: Women and Community in the Evangelical South, 1830–1900* [Chapel Hill: University of North Carolina Press, 1985] 12–13).

MEMBERSHIP STATISTICS

Church	Date Listed	M:F	Ratio	Total
Welsh Neck	1737	couples	1:1	30
Welsh Neck	1759	couples	1:1	66
Welsh Neck	1770s	separate	1:2	194
Welsh Neck	1778	separate	1:1	84
Cashaway	1756 (entry states there were 14 original members, male and female)			
Cashaway	after 1756	Couples	1:1	50
Cashaway	1767	sep/mixed	1:1	67
Mt. Pleasant	1803	sep/slaves	W1:2/B2:3	W120/B190
Reedy River	1800	sep/color	W2:3/B1:1	100/18
Sandy Run	1780s?	separate	3:4	175
			(white with free blacks)	
Sandy Run	undated	slaves mixed		130
Skewarkey	1786	separate	5:3	40
Poplar Spring	1788	separate	1:1	86
Poplar Spring	1813	separate	3:4	74
Poplar Spring	1831	separate	2:3	132
Sandy Creek	undated	separate?	1:2	71
Sandy Creek	1818	sep/ color	W1:3/B1:2	20/10
Brier Creek	1783	separate	1:1	11
Brier Creek	1822	blacks sep	2:3/?	180/21

For a while, Baptist churches in the South were composed of nearly equal numbers of men and women. During the great revival period at the century's close, however, female members began outnumbering males in most churches. What explanations might there be for this pattern? Some would suggest that women were simply more religious and more responsive to revivalism's emotional appeal. Others propose that church membership empowered women, ironically, by giving them a place in the public sphere. Church attendance was an excuse to get out of the house, interact with neighbors, and break the monotony of life. There is likely some merit in each of these theories, but one thing is clear. If women of the time saw churches as unfriendly instruments of their subjugation, one would expect them to have stayed away, at least the single women who joined churches without pressure or even support from their families. Could it be that the opposite was the case? Could women have expected to find a greater degree of fairness in churches that, to a greater extent than society, also demanded subjection of men? As will be seen in chapters 3 and 5, churches did in fact challenge Southern men to measure themselves by a higher standard.

Benedict estimates that church adherents (attendees) outnumbered communicants (members) 7:1 on average. Bonomi, however, argues that the majority of Southerners were regular churchgoers, and that the ratio of adherents to communicants was over 3:1. She suggests that gains during the Second Great Awakening were only temporary; those gains permanently widened the reach of churches into the backcountry.[30] Where membership lists and church covenant signatures are available, they are useful in determining membership patterns, although they are sometimes impossible to date precisely. Churches sometimes used the same list for several years, and not all records are dated but must be estimated based on context. Likewise, membership totals for any given year must also be estimated. Nevertheless, such documents do offer some insight into the composition of church membership.

The Cashaway Baptist Church Covenant of 1767 at first separates signatures by gender, but then mixes the two at the bottom of the list for unknown reasons. Note that Skewarkey

---

[30] Benedict, *A General History of the Baptist Denomination in America*, 2:553; Patricia Bonomi, *Under the Cope of Heaven: Religion, Society, and Politics in Colonial America* (New York: Oxford University Press, 1986) ch. 4.

Baptist stands alone with a higher ratio of male members. The temporary disruption of the gender balance at Welsh Neck Baptist Church was likely caused by the ministry of Elhanan Winchester, who baptized many converts including a disproportionate number of slaves and perhaps white women. Black members, distinguished within record book entries as "servants," were dismissed to constitute their own church around 1779. The Mt. Pleasant Baptist Church list arranges slave members by their masters, but in other churches the legal status of black members is more vague. It is possible that a few black members were free, particularly in the backcountry.

According to Heyrman, Baptist and Methodist churches separated male and female members. Whether indoor or outdoor, on the frontier or back east, "male and female members sat on opposite sides of a center aisle."[31] Seating arrangements are not described in most church records, but Skewarkey Baptist Church records reveal that men and women were divided into separate groups for the practice of foot washing. Tyger Baptist Church even assigned male and female members seats on opposite ends of the meeting house for regular meetings.[32] Another area of clear distinction is church offices. In the record books examined, not one instance can be found of a woman holding the office of pastor, lay preacher, deacon, moderator, clerk, treasurer, or messenger to another church or an association. Of course, such offices were not automatically available to men either; preachers especially had strict moral and doctrinal ordination requirements.

[31] Heyrman, *Southern Cross*, 142.

[32] *Skewarkey Baptist Church Record Book* July 1788 *Skewarkey Baptist Church Record Book*; *Tyger Baptist Church Record Book* 1810.

Women could not preach or teach in the presence of male members.[33] Their silence, however, was far from absolute, especially in church business meetings. Besides regular Sunday worship services and observance of the Lord's Supper, churches met at least monthly or quarterly for business meetings. All members, male and female, were expected to attend all meetings and participate by voting. Tyger Baptist Church's Rules of Discipline ordered absent male members to send word why they could not attend or give an excuse for themselves at the next meeting. Flat River Baptist Church affirmed in a 1786 query that it was "sensurable in a member, (especially free males) to neglect to give due attendance on church meetings, without a lawful excuse." Skewarkey Baptist Church ordered in September 1787 that the names of female members should be noted at monthly meetings just the same as males. Article 4 of the Skewarkey Baptist Church Decorum stated, "The members names being regularly enrolled shall by the clerk be distinctly called over and a significant mark put to the names of all absent members." In 1787 a man of that church cited his own wife for non-attendance. Reedy River Baptist Church in July 1805 considered the neglect of sisters in attending meetings, and resolved that "it is their duty and in case of failure to be admonished, and if still wilfully neglectful to be cited to meeting and give satisfaction for their neglect." In May of the same year, all the males and a majority of the female members of Tyger Church agreed that a list of the females be called every meeting. The next month, one brother made a motion to give the matter further consideration. In

[33] Flat River was exceptionally tolerant of the female voice when it answered a 1786 query, "What privelidges have the sisters in the church[?] Answer: It shall not be an offence if by the constraining power of God's Spirit in a time of publick Worship, they should pray or drop a word of exortation, and we believe they have an equal enterest in all matters of fellowship."

August, a sister rose and objected to the requirement that women attend; "…she thought it abominable and could not live in a church with it." The church then "labored" with the sister, showing considerable patience with her unbridled tongue.

Janet Moore Lindman highlighted episodes in Baptist churches in Philadelphia and Virginia to show that the first Great Awakening ignited a debate over a woman's "voice" in the church.[34] In 1746, the Philadelphia Baptist Association considered a query "Whether women may or ought to have their votes in the church, in such matters as the church shall agree to be decided by votes?" Women had previously enjoyed the right to vote in church business, but churches apparently saw the need to clarify the manner and extent of their participation in order to clear up any appearance of contradiction with the command for women to "keep silent." The Philadelphia Baptist Association exerted great influence on Baptist churches throughout America, maintaining correspondence with Southern associations. This record reveals so much not only about women voting in churches, but also about other ways in which their "voices" were heard.

The Association responded to the query by suggesting that women have "liberty to give a mute voice, by standing or lifting up of the hands, or the contrary, to signify their assent or dissent to the thing proposed." The response continued to explain that "absolute silence in all respects cannot be intended; for if so, how shall a woman make a confession of her faith to the satisfaction of the whole church? or how shall the church judge whether a woman be in the faith or no?" Absolute silence would also be a hindrance to the consideration of necessary testimonies in discipline trials:

---

[34] Lindman, *A World of Baptists*. Published more recently is Janet Moore Lindman, *Bodies of Belief: Baptist Community in Early America* (Philadelphia: University of Pennsylvania Press, 2011).

> How shall a woman offended, after regular private proceeding with an offending member, tell the church[?]... How shall a woman do, if she be an evidence to a matter of fact? Shall the church grope in the dark for want of her evidence to clear the doubt? Surely not. Again, how shall a woman defend herself if wrongfully accused, if she must not speak?

If, however, a woman's conscience made her uncomfortable taking advantage of such opportunities to speak for herself, the association suggested that she could still at least "make a brother a mouth to ask leave to speak, if not ask it herself." There were, nevertheless, to be limits placed upon the voices of women. The response continued, "yet ought not they to open the floodgate of speech in an imperious, tumultuous, masterly manner. Hence the silence, with subjection, enjoined on all women in the church of God, is such a silence as excludes all women whomsoever from all degrees of teaching, ruling, governing, dictating, and leading in the church of God."[35] Southern churches put into practice what the Philadelphia Baptist Association articulated in this statement. Record books show women making confessions of faith, leveling accusations, giving testimony in discipline cases, defending themselves, and sometimes opting to speak through a male representative. Women at times did "open the floodgate of speech," for which they were reproved by the church. Not once was a woman given a position of leadership in the thirty churches examined here.

Lindman also examines an incident that took place in the Philadelphia Baptist Church in 1764. Morgan Edwards, the church's new pastor, had opposed allowing female members to vote, a position which he made clear in his publication *Customs of the Primitive Churches*. When prompted by a female member, one of the deacons brought up the matter of female suffrage at a

---

[35] A. D. Gillette, *Minutes of the Philadelphia Baptist Association* (Philadelphia: American Baptist Publication Society, 1851) 1746.

business meeting. The church issued an elusive response, failing to answer the question decisively or to acknowledge that the church had done anything out of the ordinary to provoke the discussion. Joanna Anthony, one of the women involved, responded by writing a letter to the church leadership, stating that the sisters had been offended when the pastor recently left out the female members in the election of church deacons. According to this letter, the women wanted the church to consider the matter of their suffrage being denied. Some of the men had phrased the query so as to question whether their right to suffrage existed and to ignore the incident that provoked their dissatisfaction. Anthony wrote, "We know our former rights and we beg to know who had a right to deprive us of them." In response to her letter, at the next business meeting the men of the church voted 12:4 that "the women should be allowed to give their suffrage as heretofore." Even in a church led by a pastor such as Morgan Edwards, the sisters were able to successfully defend their traditional right to vote.

Lindman and Susan Juster both suggest that women lost their ability to vote on church matters around the end of the eighteenth century. Lindman finds several scattered examples of Virginia associations and churches placing restrictions on female church suffrage, especially in the last decades of the eighteenth century. For example, some limited their suffrage to certain types of issues, and others issued vague statements that their power was not equal to that of the men, but very few examples are offered of churches overturning female suffrage altogether in the Carolinas. Juster claims that New England churches abandoned female suffrage in the 1790s. Whether or not Juster and Lindman exaggerated the extent to which churches in New England and Virginia reversed their policy of female suffrage at that time, church records from the Carolinas show no indication of such a shift. The records from the Carolinas surveyed here indicate no decline in the privilege women enjoyed earlier in the eighteenth century.[36]

In addition to female suffrage, more evidence is found in church records of the Carolinas to clarify the limited yet significant participation of women in church affairs. Records often mention a "door being open" for reception of new members at these meetings. It was also a time for granting letters of dismissal to other churches, considering members under discipline, and discussing financial business. When couples or families requested admission or dismissal together, the husbands frequently spoke for their families.[37] Women, however, often joined and left churches on their own. Especially when presenting themselves for baptism, women were often heard relating their conversion experience before the church. Article 5 of the Skewarkey Baptist Church Decorum describes that church's customary manner of receiving new members:

> A Door shall be opened (when thought necessary) for the admission of new members into the church, but none shall be admitted but by unanimous consent, and shall first verbally relate their experience or give an account of the work of God on their souls and secondly of their faith and principles (if the church shall require it) and thirdly the church shall make diligent inquiry respecting their moral conduct, and when full

---

[36] Lindman, *A World of Baptists*, 155–58; Susan Juster, *Disorderly Women: Sexual Politics and Evangelicalism in Revolutionary New England* (Ithaca: Cornell University Press, 1994). See also Cornelia Hughes Dayton, *Women Before the Bar: Gender, Law, and Society in Connecticut, 1639–1789* (Chapel Hill: University of North Carolina Press, 1995). Dayton argues that Connecticut courtrooms allowed women more participation in the seventeenth century, when Puritanism held men and women accountable for their actions on a surprisingly equal footing. In the eighteenth century, however, the strength of Puritanism gave way to secular courtrooms with more bias towards women.

[37] See ch. 2 for examples.

> satisfaction shall be obtained the Pastor, Deacon or Moderator shall manifest the same by first giving them the right hand of fellowship, and thereby receiving them in form.

Women joined churches in the same ways as men. If never before baptized, they made a public confession of faith before the church and requested baptism. Upon being received as members, they were welcomed into the church with the "right hand of fellowship." If transferring from another church, they presented letters of recommendation from the former church or explained why such a letter was not available. If moving to another church, they were expected to request regular dismissal and recommendation; otherwise they would be considered leaving "in disorder."

As will be seen in chapter four, women sometimes also participated alongside men in the financial business of churches. But perhaps the most striking evidence of a woman's "voice" is to be found in church discipline cases. As before mentioned, the "voice" of female church members was restricted. Article 10 Section 9 of the Skewarkey Baptist Church Decorum stated, "The Woman hath not a right by the law of Christ to usurp Authority over the man and therefore ought not to speak in the Church only in cases of conscience or in such particular circumstances that the nature of the thing may require it." The Kehukee Baptist Association reached the same conclusion in a query of 1784.[38] What then were the "particular circumstances" in which a woman's voice was permitted?

---

[38] The query read, "Has a woman any right to speak in the church in matters of discipline unless called upon? Answer: We think they have no right unless called upon, or where it respects their own communion" (C. B. Hassell and S. Hassell, *History of the Church of God* [1886; repr., Ellenwood GA: Old School Hymnal Co., 1983] 831).

When did women exercise a voice in church business? "Cases of conscience" were most likely to be found in discipline cases. Women were sometimes appointed as "messengers" to disorderly members. This was more common in cases involving other women, but sometimes a wife was sent as a messenger to her husband as well. Tyger Baptist Church, in its Rules of Church Discipline, ordered that female members should not be called on as "helps" except in some cases related to females. When a woman was accused of an offense, the church requested that she appear to testify in her own behalf, just as a man would. Women also testified in behalf of others, and in some discipline cases, women were found charging men with allegations of misconduct.[39] In fact, men and women were specifically exhorted to express their dissatisfaction if they were offended by another member or by the church as a whole. The Skewarkey Baptist Church Decorum stated that "Any member being grieved at any thing done in conference and shall hold his or her peace and shall not let the same be known, until Conference rises And shall afterwards speak of the same (as it manifestly tends to confusion) it is hereby deemed disorder." And Eaton Baptist Church agreed in 1773 that all members were at liberty to speak out (one at a time) and express their dissatisfaction. As will be seen in the next chapter, brothers and sisters were often seen taking advantage of their right to express dissatisfaction with each other.[40]

What churches taught concerning the subjection of women must be understood within the context of a larger system of subjection, a moral economy with expectations for men and women, parents and children, masters and servants, and entire church congregations. Furthermore, this doctrine was not peculiar to

---

[39] See examples in chs. 2 and 4 of accusations of gossiping, cursing, and breaking financial contracts.

[40] See Skewarkey Decorum, Article 10, Sections 9 and 6.

Baptists in the Carolinas. It was recognized in the writings of a diverse array of religious leaders and was likely a part of everyday practice in most churches (although inadequate records preclude certainty). While the secular world was less rigid in enforcing the subjection of women and especially men, churches had no monopoly on the ideology of subjection. Women did not have the same roles as men in church business, but they did have a significant "place" of their own that should not be overlooked. Discipline cases gave them a particularly revealing stage upon which to exercise their "voices." If their subjection involved an oppressive double standard, one would expect it to be most evident in the discipline cases, where church members were put on trial for allegations of misconduct. One would expect business meetings to prove courts of gross injustice in their discrimination against women. As will be seen, such is not the case.

2

UNITY AND DISCORD

Several historians have argued that discipline within Baptist churches from New England to the American South can be broken down into gendered categories. Among them are Susan Juster, Jane Kamensky, and Janet Moore Lindman. According to Juster, female church members in New England were increasingly marginalized in the late eighteenth century as "sin became a gendered construct." She suggests that women were routinely excommunicated for sins of "disorder" such as slander, lying, and fornication, and "feminine" qualities in general came to define the very essence of sin. After statistically examining discipline cases for various categories of offenses, she concludes that "A striking feature of church discipline in the mid-eighteenth century is the extent to which it was applied equally to men and women," at least in cases of "sins against the community." She continues, however, by arguing that there were "sharp and distinct" gender patterns in certain categories of offenses: "Women were far more likely to be disciplined for sexual misconduct and sins against family/household, while men were disciplined in greater numbers for sins of avarice, fighting or quarreling with neighbors, and drunkenness."[1]

Kamensky reached a similar conclusion after examining seventeenth-century New England court records. According to Kamensky, New Englanders in general recognized the importance of maintaining the proper balance between speaking with "freedom" and "restraint." But especially after prominent trials involving women such as Anne Hutchinson, Ann Hibbens, and those accused of witchcraft later in the century, the female tongue came to be governed with particular care.[2]

In her examination of Virginia and Pennsylvania Baptists, Lindman divides offenses into three categories: religious (truancy, heresy), social (drunkenness, carnality, language), and sexual (fornication, adultery). According to Lindman, "Though men and women, blacks and whites, were accused of similar offenses, the specific type of indiscretion one was accused of...was usually indicative of one's place in society." White men were most likely to be charged with social offenses, white women with religious offenses, and black men and women of sexual offenses. Lindman suggests that discipline was carried out more rigorously in Virginia than in Pennsylvania, especially against black members, but that it gradually declined everywhere, especially with regard to female members.[3]

If Juster, Kamensky, and Lindman are correct in their assessment of discipline patterns in eighteenth-century New

---

[1] Susan Juster, *Disorderly Women: Sexual Politics and Evangelicalism in Revolutionary New England* (Ithaca: Cornell University Press, 1994) 8, 106.

[2] Jane Kamensky, *Governing the Tongue: The Politics of Speech in Early New England* (New York: Oxford University Press, 1997).

[3] Janet Moore Lindman, *A World of Baptists: Gender, Race, and Religious Community in Pennsylvania and Virginia, 1689–1825* (Minneapolis: University of Minnesota, 1994) 210–13, 235.

England, Pennsylvania, and Virginia, then churches in the Carolinas do not fit the model seen elsewhere. The records under consideration here do not support the theory that the position of women in churches was undergoing change during the eighteenth century, which should raise doubts about the validity of the claim for other regions. Baptist church records from the Carolinas do show that men and women were represented disproportionately for a few offenses, as will be seen in the next chapter. Nevertheless, discipline cases dealing with non-attendance, general contention, sins of the tongue, and heresy suggest that women received equal (or occasionally special) treatment, with few exceptions.[4]

Church records show how members often fell short of the ideal of church fellowship set forth in Scripture, and how churches responded to the breach of their covenants. Churches sometimes adopted written covenants, articles of faith, rules of discipline, and rules of decorum. These documents reveal much about church practice and doctrine. Such church documents were often very similar in content to one another, and association documents reflected this unity. The Charleston Baptist Association, for example, summarized proper discipline procedure in its *Summary of Church Discipline*; churches were to

---

[4] Terri Snyder finds evidence in Virginia court records that women used their tongues to effectively challenge patriarchy during the seventeenth century. Snyder suggests that the voices of women were increasingly censured by civil law during the eighteenth century, after a period of social flux with demographic imbalance, indentured servitude (*Brabbling Women: Disorderly Speech and the Law in Early Virginia* [London: Cornell University Press, 2003]). See also Lois Carr and Lorena Walsh, "The Planter's Wife: The Experience of White Women in Seventeenth-Century Maryland," *William and Mary Quarterly*, 3d ser., 34 (1977).

rebuke, suspend, and excommunicate wayward members (in that order) when duty demanded it.[5]

Church covenants and rules of decorum were very similar throughout the Kehukee Baptist Association. In the Skewarkey Baptist Church Covenant of 1789, members pledged that they would no longer consider themselves their own, but rather they all belonged to God and to each other. They furthermore resolved to "give [them]selves to oneanother [*sic*] and receive oneanother [*sic*] in the Lord" as "one body." They then promised to assemble together, maintain discipline, and to "love as brethren and submit to oneanother in the Lord."[6] The example church covenant reprinted in the association's history is nearly identical to the one found in the Skewarkey record book for 1806. In this version, the church reaffirmed that they had "given up [them]selves to the Lord, and to one another, in a gospel church way, to be governed and guided by a proper discipline…in the most brotherly affection towards each other." They then promised more specifically "In brotherly love to pray for each other, to watch over one another, and, if need be, in the most tender and affectionate manner, to reprove one another." They furthermore agreed,

> with God's assistance, to pray in [their] families, attend [their] church meetings, observe the Lord's day and keep it holy, and not absent [them]selves from the communion of the Lord's Supper without a lawful excuse; to be ready to communicate to the defraying of the church's expenses, and for the support of the ministry; not irregularly depart from the fellowship of the

---

[5] Baptist Associations, with the exception of the more powerful early Sandy Creek Association, were advisory bodies composed of representatives from independent churches (Charleston Baptist Association, *Summary of Church Discipline* [Charleston: CBA, 1783] ch. 1).

[6] Skewarkey Covenant, 1789.

church, nor to remove to distant churches without a regular dismission.[7]

Cashaway, and later Mechanicsville, adopted similar covenants in South Carolina. Cashaway covenanted in 1767 that they esteemed it their "Duty to walk with each other in all Humility and Brotherly Love to watch over each others Conversation," assemble together, and "as the Case requires to warn, rebuke, and admonish one another." They promised to "sympathize with each other," to "bear with one anothers Weaknesses, Failings, Infirmities and perticulerly [*sic*] to pray for one another," and to keep the secrets of the Church as a "Garden enclosed."[8] The members of Mechanicsville promised in Article 9 of their covenant to hold themselves "censurable for evil speaking, either irreverently of God, or to the prejudice of our brethren with whom [they] ought to maintain fellowship in the church." They also promised not to expose the faults or weaknesses of brethren to anyone "unless necessary to reclaim from error or sin."[9] Black Creek members pledged in their church covenant to "give up [them]selves to the Lord and likewise to one another by the will of God," and to "walk with each other in all humility and brotherly love to watch over each others conversation to stir up one another to love and good works not forsaking the assembling of ourselves together…to sympathise with each other in all conditions…."

As other churches, the members of Tyger Baptist Church pledged in their Covenant that they were "no longer [their] own," and that they did "voluntarily and freely give

[7] C. B. Hassell and S. Hassell, *History of the Church of God* (1886; repr., Ellenwood GA: Old School Hymnal Co., 1983) 695; Skewarkey Covenant, 1806.

[8] Cashaway Articles of Faith and Church Covenant, Articles 15–17, 1767.

[9] Mechanicsville Church Covenant, Article 9.

[them]selves one to another in the Lord," uniting as a "distinct body," and promising to "assemble together on all convenient oppertuninies [*sic*]," "Love as brethren" and "submit to each other." Tyger's record book also contains many discipline cases in which members broke such promises made to one another. The most common type of discipline case was for non-attendance. Fellow members were "wounded" by brethren and sisters who were frequently "out of duty" by missing worship services, church meetings, and ordinances, or who "moved away disorderly" by not requesting regular dismissal from the membership. Since church members were all members of one "body," all parts of the whole, whether male or female, were essential to church fellowship. If a brother or sister neglected church attendance, the body could not function at full capacity; it was as though an arm or a leg or a finger were missing. But a member could also disrupt church unity without neglecting to attend. Similar to a foot out of joint, a troublesome member could cause the church body trouble without deserting it. In addition to non-attendance, another threat to brotherly unity was the tongues of members. Bickering, vulgar language, gossip, lies, heresy, and general contention could break church fellow-ship. Such behavior was equally unacceptable in male or female members, for they were to be one in Christ.

Roaring River agreed in 1786 to reprove members who neglected church meetings without sending "a lawful excuse" or attending the next meeting. In 1792, the church ordered that when male members missed monthly meetings without sending an excuse, the church would appoint delegates to inquire into the matter. In 1795, the policies were put to the test. Gibson Maner[10] was cited in May to explain "why he would pass by the

[10] This name is also spelled "Mainor" and "Mainard" in other places.

meeting house on church meeting day and not attend meeting." At the same time, John Sparks was also cited for neglecting attendance. In June, the two men "both left the place before the church got together." In July, report was made that Sparks had said that "he had as leave be out of the church as in it," for which he was excommunicated. In September, Maner's wife Sarah expressed dissatisfaction that the church "shut out" her husband as well. The church tried to convince her that the action was appropriate, but in October she openly denounced the church's action in "cuting off" her husband. In November she herself was excommunicated. Flat River insisted in 1786 that it was mandatory for members, "especially free males" to attend meetings. And Lick Fork resolved in 1811 that "every member missing church meeting shall on the next meeting make his excuse."

Throughout Skewarkey Baptist Church's records there are frequent complaints of non-attendance. In 1798, Brier Creek excommunicated a man for persistent absence and "railing" against the church. In September 1787, a Skewarkey man motioned "that if any brother or sister be absent so long that any of the other members are wounded that they make the same known to the Deacons and they to the church." Poplar Springs often cited, and sometimes excommunicated, both male and female members for nonattendance, especially around the turn of the century.[11] The church was also wounded when members failed to partake of the Lord's Supper. In June 1746, Ashley River sent messengers to a man for "neglecting his place at the Lord's Table." Lick Fork in 1798 demanded that "a member not receiving the sacrament" must give reasons for abstaining. Skewarkey agreed in December 1803 that members refusing to

[11] See cases in 1797,1799, 1800, 1803–1806.

partake of the elements should render their reasons.[12] Absence from church meetings and ordinances signified disunity. Such behavior "wounded" other members, whether because of simple negligence or open contempt, as in the 1802 Brier Creek case of a husband and wife who were excommunicated "for disorder in leaving meeting and taking their daughter off when the church was giving her advice."

When relocating, church members were expected to ask the church for a regular letter of dismissal recommending them to another church "of like faith and order." But members sometimes disregarded the authority of a church by abandoning it without permission.[13] In November 1804, Jersey excommunicated a man for "being moved out of the place and for not going according to the rules of the church." The same church excommunicated another man in June 1809 for "going away in disorder." Lick Fork excommunicated a man in 1805 for leaving

---

[12] The Kehukee Association answered the following query in 1782: "What shall a church do with a member who shall absent himself from the communion of the Lord's Supper? Answer: That it is the duty of the church to inquire into the reason of his thus absenting himself from the communion, and if he does not render satisfactory reasons, the church shall deal with him" (Hassell and Hassell, *History of the Church of God*, 830).

[13] The Kehukee Association considered the following query in 1782: "What method shall be taken with a member who shall rend himself off from his own church and join another? Answer: We think it is disorderly for a member to rend himself off from his own church, and disorderly for a church to receive him." In 1824, it answered another: "Is it agreeable to gospel order for members of a Baptist Church to withdraw themselves from the church to which they belong, or join another of the same faith and order, without a regular dismission? or for another church to receive such members without such dismission? Answer: On gospel principles we think that in each case it is wrong" (ibid., 830, 834).

in disorder. In December 1803, Skewarkey excommunicated a man for "removing without a regular request for dismissal." In September 1809, Reedy River excommunicated a man "for moving away in disorder," but retained his wife in fellowship. The details of this case are unknown, but one can speculate that the circumstances may well have been beyond the wife's control since her husband made the decision to move the family.

The Poplar Spring records for the same time period also contain several examples of regular dismissal policy. Sometimes husbands petitioned for dismissal in behalf of themselves and their wives, as was the case in 1804, 1806, and 1818. In 1803 a woman petitioned by way of a man with a different last name, but in 1820 another woman presented her own petition for dismissal. Roaring River likewise had frequent requests for dismissal, sometimes by couples and sometimes by individuals. This was especially common around 1795, when many of the members were relocating to Kentucky. Whether a woman spoke for herself in such matters seems to have depended upon marital status and personal preference. If a married woman joined a church along with her husband, it was customary for her husband to request admission on behalf of them both. But women who were either single or joining a church independently of their husbands appear to have had the option of requesting admission themselves or asking a man of the church to speak for them.

In February 1806, Jersey passed a resolution to "inquire for fellowship every meeting" to determine whether there was peace among the members. As the records show, such inquiries often received disappointing answers in every church. Some discipline cases are vague and are best described as "general contention." A few patterns surface upon examination of these cases as a category. Out of more than sixty such cases, men were twice as likely to be charged being contentious." As illustrated in the graph below, half of the "contention cases" involved disputes between men alone, a third of the cases involved both men and women, and a sixth involved women only. One quarter of those charged also faced excommunication. Eleven males and four females were excommunicated; since twice as many men were charged, it should be no surprise that a disproportionate number were excommunicated. Churches sometimes arbitrated disputes, occasionally appointing committees or presbyteries to investigate the circumstances. But in other cases, parties were ordered to settle disputes between themselves.[14]

A good example of contention is found in Cashaway's Sister Jameson, who was repeatedly suspended and restored in the 1760s and 1770s for disputes with both male and female members. In 1815, two Reedy River sisters with an "unfellowship" between them were "sent out to talk in private and they returned reconsiled." Later that year, two other sisters of the church reported reconciliation when the one at fault gave satisfaction, but the confessor's husband was excommunicated for getting angry over the church's dealings with his wife. In 1806, Tyger likewise "laid it on" two brethren "to settle it there selves, accordingly done." In 1801, Brier Creek dealt for several months with a dispute between a brother and sister. The man first "laid in a grievance" against the woman, and she was "found guilty with a hard Spirit." The case was laid over, and she later appeared and was restored after begging for forgiveness. The same month, however, the two came before the

[14] Another Kehukee Association query of 1822 read, "How shall a church proceed, who knows that two of her members are not in fellowship with each other? Answer: Let the parties comply with the directions given in the eighteenth chapter of St. Matthew's gospel; and should they refuse to comply, and yet be unreconciled, let them be called before the church, and the church enter into an investigation of the subject or matter of difference, and deal with the parties as they appear to deserve" (ibid., 834).

church again with yet another "contradiction"; "both appeared to have a very hard spirit against each other." The next month both were censured, and the month after that the woman said she might be mistaken, and finally "acknowledged that she had sinned and it might be as [he] said but could not remember it." The next month, they both acknowledged their faults and offered one another handshakes of fellowship. These cases illustrate the effectiveness of church arbitration in disputes between members. Such arbitration, however, did not always successfully satisfy contentious members. A woman of Cashie lashed out at other members when cited to answer an inquiry in church conference in 1793. According to the clerk's records, the sister "expressed her self with so much acrimony to the great grief of the Church" and when she and her daughter requested that their names be removed from the church book, the church unanimously granted their requests. Turkey Creek excommunicated a man in 1801 for "raising a quarrel" with another brother and "refusing to go and make peace" with him or attend church meeting when cited to answer for his conduct.

In 1788, Skewarkey witnessed a case of some "great discord" between three men and one woman in which all were tried separately and excommunicated. But the records of discipline cases make it clear that churches sought, and usually achieved, reconciliation instead of excommunication. Again and again, churches demonstrated patience with male and female members in their attempts to restore harmony among members. When excommunications did occur, it was usually done reluctantly when the accused remained obstinate, leaving the church no other remedy. Why cases of general contention most often involved male members is uncertain. Maybe they were simply more contentious. Maybe they were bolder in confronting one another. Only one thing is clear: this type of discipline case concentrated disproportionately on men, a fact that should raise doubts about the alleged discrimination of church discipline against women.

Many cases of contention are more specific and more evenly distributed among men and women. Charges and excommunications for gossip were equal for men and women, and about half of those disciplined were excommunicated. Gossip cases included charges of defamation, "villifying" other members, speaking evil of the church or pastor, whispering, slandering, ridiculing, railing, and making false accusations.[15] Tyger dealt with Sister Hannah Belew[16] in 1806 for "having ungodly talk against the church." What she said against the church is not recorded, but she gave satisfaction and was kept in fellowship. The next year, however, a brother "laid in a charge in behalf of the church" against her. The records are again unclear about the nature of his charge, but it may have been related to her application for financial support that was being considered at the time. Whatever the charge, "when inquisition was made she flew into a violent passion and charg[ed] the church," for which she was censured. The following year, she was once again a source of contention. This time the church finally excluded the sister, but one month later it took her back upon her recantation. Then in 1810, she came under discipline again, and when she "sent word that she was nothing but a fustiment to the church," she was once again excommunicated.

As demonstrated by Sister Belew, a woman who repeatedly spoke out against the church could meet with considerable tolerance. Churches were willing to forgive, but not overlook, such offenses. When members refused to repent of their sins of

---

[15] Women convicted of slander and gossip were sometimes punished by ducking and other methods in colonial America. See Julia Cherry Spruill, *Women's Life and Work in the Southern Colonies* (Chapel Hill: University of North Carolina Press, 1938) 330.

[16] See Belew family cases in ch. 4.

the tongue, however, excommunication was considered necessary to restore harmony. A Brier Creek man accused a woman in 1805 with "speaking evil of one of his daughters." The woman appeared "with a very hard spirit and unbecoming words and desired to be excommunicated," which was done. In this case, the defendant refused to repent and slighted the opportunity for restoration. Another case in which a woman was excommunicated was when a woman of Turkey Creek in 1785 was dealt with for "speaking disrespectful of the brethren also for disowning the truth and for busying herself in matters that she ought not with young people." Other cases resulting in a woman's excommunication involved "villification" and speaking against the church or another female member. Men were excommunicated for slander compounded by drunkenness or ridicule, and "railing against the church." On the other hand, several men and women appear to have avoided excommunication when accused of defamation, whether against a pastor or a fellow member of either sex. The rarity of gossip cases is striking; only Brier Creek reported multiple cases, most of which involved male defendants. Perhaps the distinction churches made between "watching over" one another and gossiping reserved only the most obvious cases of abuse for disciplinary action.

GOSSIP CASES

D	Church	Year	Offense	Ex
F	Welsh Neck	1767	defamation	
F	Ashley River	1737	speaking evil of pastor	
F	Eaton's	1787	relating report about F	
BF	Turkey Creek	1809	slander	
F	Cashaway	1769–70	villification	X
F	Tyger	1806/07/10	ungodly talk against church	X
F	Brier Creek	1805	speaking evil of F	X

D	Church	Year	Offense	Ex
F	Turkey Creek	1785	disrespect, busybody	X
Females Charged:		8	Excommunicated:	4
M	Reedy River	1814	accused by F of whispering	
M	Brier Creek	1807	accused F of slave abuse	
M	Clear Springs	1813	defamation	
M	Brier Creek	1793	speaking evil of members	
M	Brier Creek	1794	slander/drunkenness	X
M/M	Brier Creek	1797	slander/ridicule	X (1)
M	Brier Creek	1798	railing against church	X
Males	Charged:	8	Excommunicated: 3	

D=Defendant
M=male defendant; F=female defendant; B=black defendant;
EX=excommunication

Another category of contention cases involves offensive language. Specific examples include cursing, swearing, and profanity, as well as language considered abusive, ill, harsh, or disorderly. Only slightly more men were charged with this type of offense. One might expect to find that more males were cited for using inappropriate language or that female defendants were more likely to be excommunicated for this type of offense. Men had the more notorious reputation for cursing and swearing, and women for holding their tongues, but apparently the difference was not significant enough to reflect on discipline statistics. Just under half of the men and women who were charged were excommunicated.[17] Although the cases are few, there does appear to be a pattern in the type of case that was most likely to result in excommunication. The excommunications were for "profanity," "cursing," "swearing," and taking God's name in vain while charges of language that was "rude," "abusive," "disorderly," "harsh," or "ill" were forgiven. The content of inappropriate language seems to have been taken more seriously than the spirit with which it was uttered. A temper was bad, but to express it with taboo terminology was worse.

In most instances, the records do not give detailed accounts of what was said, but there are rare and colorful exceptions. A woman of Turkey Creek, for example, in 1804 exclaimed in reference to a man who had somehow upset her, "give [him] to the Devil, and let him eat him." The same year, Brother Roberts of Bush River, a preacher, was charged with "using extremely vulgar language which modesty forbids to mention here and it was thought necessary for the sake of modesty for the male members to withdraw for the purpose of inquiring into the nature of the case." Brother Roberts confessed to the charge, and the church "thought necessary to silence him from using a publick gift," but he was allowed to remain "a private member." When a man of Gum Branch was accused of swearing by men who were not members of the church, their evidence was considered unsatisfactory. When no additional evidence was produced the church agreed to restore him to fellowship.

---

[17] An insane woman whose behavior Skewarkey agreed to overlook in 1807 was excommunicated in 1811 for "repeatedly using profane language."

LANGUAGE CASES

D	Church	Year	Charge	EX
F	Welsh Neck	1761	abusive language	
F/F	Skewarkey	1789	disorderly conduct	
F	Turkey Creek	1804	cursed M?	
F	Turkey Creek	1809	profane swearing?	
F	Bush River	1806	swear/God's name in vain	X
F	Skewarkey	1807/11	repeated profanity	X
M	Brier Creek	1807	harsh words	
M	Ashley River	1739	ill words	
M	Turkey Creek	1803	spoke rudely to F while drunk	
BM	Turkey Creek	1807	spoke rudely to F	
M	Lick Fork	1794	backbiting	
M	Bush River	1804	preacher's vulgarity	
M	Gum Branch	1796	swearing	
M	Bush River	1806	swear, quarrel, drunk	X
M	Sandy Creek	1817/21	charged by F with cursing	X
M	Reedy River	1809	swearing, etc.	X

D=Defendant
EX=Excommunicate

In other cases, members were disciplined for telling lies. Occasionally, excommunicated women were more specifically accused of "making mischief" in the community with their falsehood.[18] Since this phrase was only used in reference to female offenders, falsehood that threatened community order may have been a gender-specific concern. But for falsehood cases in general, men were much more likely to be charged, and approximately two thirds of those charged were excommuni-

[18] See Brier Creek 1802–1803.

cated. An exception to the balanced pattern followed by most discipline cases, here members do appear to have been convicted disproportionately by gender. Although fewer women were charged with falsehood, those charged were more likely to be excommunicated than men; in fact, all women and black members who were charged with the offense were excommunicated. At first glance, it might appear that women and black members met with less leniency than men, but it is also possible that they were only charged with more serious offenses while lesser ones were overlooked. Individual cases suggest that some lies were taken more seriously than others, especially those which were intended to cover up another offense.

Bush River offers several good examples for the year 1805. One woman was excommunicated for getting drunk and lying in her assertion that it was her first such offense. According to the church, it had been proven otherwise and she was "not at present a fit member of society." Another woman had a man excommunicated the previous year by testifying that he had raped her. But in 1805, she herself was excommunicated after retracting her accusation and swearing before authorities that "she was compelled to swear against [him] [that is, they made her lie about being raped]; as above by her husband and his father and her husbands brother which she saith on her oath that she did believe it was the effects of a malicious spirit with an intention to take his life." Such lies were serious matters, as were those for which men faced excommunication. The preacher who was silenced from preaching months earlier for vulgar language then claimed that he had an affair with a woman of the church before either of them became members. When she denied his assertion that he "at will enjoyed her in a carnal manner," the church called for "helps" and decided to excommunicate him. The same year, another man of that church was excommunicated for adultery compounded by "wilful falsity to hide his sin." It is likely that the lies for which men escaped excommunication were usually less consequential than this cover-up.

Falsehood Cases

Defendant	Church	Year	Excommunication
BF	Clear Springs	1806	X
BF	Clear Springs	1812	X
F	Skewarkey	1804	X
F	Skewarkey	1805	X
F	Brier Creek	1796	X
F	Brier Creek	1802	X
F	Brier Creek	1803	X
F	Brier Creek	1803	X
F	Brier Creek	1807/08	X
F	Roaring River	1790	X
F	Turkey Creek	1808	X
F	Bush River	1805	X
F	Bush River	1805	X

13/13 female defendants excommunicated

M	Roaring River	1790	X
BM	Skewarkey	1812/13	X
M	Jersey	1812	X
M	Roaring River	1787	X
M	Eaton's	1775/76	X
M	Skewarkey	1803	X
M	Skewarkey	1804	X
M	Bush River	1804-05	X
M	Bush River	1805	X
M/M	Skewarkey	1807	X (1)
M	Reedy River	1804	
M	Jersey	1804	
M/M	Jersey	1805	

M	Brier Creek	1803
M	Roaring River	1787
M	Roaring River	1789
M	Eaton's	1779?
M	Poplar Springs	1788/89
M	Lick Fork	1805
M	Lick Fork	1816
M	Wheeley's	1792

10/23 male defendants excommunicated

Nearly twice as many men were examined by the churches, but the excommunication rate was nearly the same for men and women. It may be that half of the falsehood cases against men were of less consequence or more easily resolved than the others.

A final category of contention is heresy. Some of these cases are doctrinal, some concern church authority, and others are vague in nature. The most common doctrinal heresy had to do with denying the concept of "election," that is, the fundamental doctrine that God had elected only certain people to salvation.[19] Anyone who disputed "election" was guilty of heresy. Skewarkey ordered in 1787 that "difference of opinions in fundamentals" was a bar to communion. The doctrine of election was one such fundamental doctrine; when asked for confirmation in 1791, no member of the church objected to the doctrine. In 1793, when a brother asked the church for permission to "ly mute for

[19] In 1799 the Kehukee Association answered the following query: "Is it right for a church in this Association to hold in fellowship a member who openly avows the Arminian tenents, or that person should be appointed a delegate to the Association to represent the church in its deliberations? Answer: We suppose it is not right to hold such person in fellowship, and therefore of course it would be improper to appoint him a delegate to the Association" (Hassell and Hassell, *History of the Church of God*, 833).

six months" to consider the doctrine, several members were "agrieved by his conduct." He asked to have his name removed from the membership list and was accordingly excommunicated. In 1789 the church unanimously barred a traveling preacher who believed in universal restoration (i.e., that God would eventually save the entire human race, not just an elect few), and an 1803 query once again confirmed the church's belief in election. A belief in "universal restoration" was considered more extreme than belief in "universal atonement," which made salvation a possibility for anyone who would claim it. Eaton's suspended a man in 1791 for advocating universal redemption but restored him after he repented. In 1800, Reedy River excommunicated a man for holding to the "universal system." Welsh Neck pastor Elhanan Winchester, who had come under scrutiny for baptizing many "converts" who showed little evidence of the new birth, became notorious for openly teaching "universalism" after leaving the South.

Universalists certainly did not have a monopoly on heresy. In 1746, Ashley River suspended a man for denying that the physical senses existed in heaven and hell. Eaton's questioned a man in 1784 concerning his claim to the gift of prophecy, but the man apparently proved to the church's satisfaction that, rather than making a heretical claim, he was indeed gifted. In a similar 1787 case, Roaring River questioned a man's assertion that he could read the entire Bible "by head…without the book," but the church "could not disprove" his claim. Other heresy cases are more vague. Poplar Spring excommunicated a woman in 1794 for "departing from the truth," and Clear Spring excommunicated a man and a woman for unclear heresies in 1806. In 1787, Skewarkey questioned the propriety of holding opinions not supported by Scripture, and Tyger ordered in 1803 that members consult with the elders before introducing strange new things to the church.

Heresy also came in the form of insulting the reputation of Baptist churches. In 1779, for example, Eaton's called upon a "Mr. Hill's church" to answer for administering the Lord's Supper to members it had excluded. The offending church apologized for its action and agreed to recognize the validity of Eaton's disciplinary actions in the future. And in 1807, Reedy River answered a letter from a church in Indiana Territory relating the recantation of an excluded member by insisting, "if he has one [a recantation] to make, here is the proper place to make it."

Problems also arose from members visiting, sharing the Lord's Supper with, or recognizing baptisms of churches of other denominations.[20] In 1794 Lick Fork answered a query by confirming that a person "baptised by a Methodist in our mode" must be re-baptized in order to join the church. In 1805 Eaton's answered a query regarding whether members of a Baptist church should commune with other denominations by saying the practice was "not agreeable to order." The church then excluded a woman for "breaking through the rules of the church by communing with other denominations." In 1804 Poplar Spring excommunicated a man for, among other offenses, "disorderly leaving the church for a different society." In 1811

---

[20] Note the following queries of the Kehukee Association: "Is it right for the ministers or the members of the Baptist denomination to publish meetings for preaching for such whose religious principles or practices they have no fellowship with? Answer: No" (1807); "Is it thought disorderly in a member of one of our churches to attend the preaching of such persons as may be excommunicated from other churches of the same faith and order? Answer: The Association give it as their opinion that, as it highly favors confusion, it would be disorderly" (1809); "Is it according to gospel order for any member or church of our Association to invite into our pulpits, to preach, any minister of any other order? Answer: No" (1834) (ibid., 833–34).

Tyger rejected a man's request to commune with Presbyterians and Methodists. In 1806 Reedy River declared that it was not "Christian prudence" for members to hear excommunicated or disorderly preachers, and in 1815 the same church again declared that it was disorderly for Baptist church members to hear preachers who were deemed disorderly, excommunicated, or simply not in fellowship with Baptist churches. In 1789 Skewarkey advised a man against hearing "heterodox principles advanced."[21] Several churches excommunicated members for their ecumenism, usually in joining with the Methodists.

[21] Baptist churches did not always prohibit interdenominational fellowship. Reedy River allowed ministers of other denominations to preach for a few months in 1817 before retracting the decision. In 1761 Welsh Neck briefly experimented with open communion and in 1782 began to admit interdenominational preachers. Clear Spring postponed a regular meeting in 1813 to avoid conflicting with a Methodist camp meeting. In addition to other denominations of churches, Baptists were also divided concerning fellowship with Freemasonry. Many churches prohibited members from becoming Masons, but Clear Spring declared in 1805 that, "None of our members shall join with a Masonic Lodge without first asking leave of the church."

HERESY CASES

D	Church	Year	Offense	P
M	Lick Fork	1792	ecumenism	(expressed confusion)
M	Brushy Creek	1799	deny Sabbath	(deal with him)
M	Eaton's	1791	universalism	suspended/ restored
M	Ashley River	1746	heaven/hell	suspended
M(4)	Yadkin	1894	general atonement	X(half)
M	Skewarkey	1793	questioning election	X
M	Reedy River	1800	universalism	X
M	Poplar Springs	1804	ecumenism	X
M	Clear Springs	1806	vague	X
M/F	Lick Fork	1816	ecumenism	X(both)
F	Bush River	1826	ecumenism	X
F	Bush River	1804	universal redemption	X
F	Turkey Creek	1794	ecumenism	X
F	Clear Springs	1806	vague	X
F	Poplar Springs	1794	vague	X
F	Eaton's	1805	ecumenism	X
F	Roaring River	1797	visions	X

D=Defendant

X=Excommunicated

7/13 males excommunicated; 8/8 women excommunicated

As with falsehood cases, men were twice as likely to be charged with heresy, but they were excommunicated at nearly the same rate as women. The men appear to have been more likely to express heretical views but also more likely to abandon them and be restored to fellowship.

Baptist historian David Benedict recorded an anecdote illustrating how women sometimes led charges in the fight against heresy. While visiting churches in the Yadkin Association, Joseph Murphy

> was once opposed by a fanatick of more effrontery than argument, who contended that Adam, before his fall, had not a mortal body, but was a pure spiritual being. A woman was sitting by, carelessly nursing her child, whose name was Frost, who said to the opposer, "I do not see how God could take out a rib from Adam's side, and close up the *flesh* again, if he were nothing but a *spirit*." "Ah," replied Mr. Murphy, "I think, my friend [meaning the "fanatick"], you are *frost*-bitten, and will soon wither without any arguments of mine."[22]

Here a minister was commending a woman for championing orthodoxy by putting a heretical man to shame. The minister considered this a permissible use of the female voice—as long, of course, as she was on the right side of the debate.

Overall, more men were accused of heresy. Few members were disciplined for this offense, but of those few, all the women and half the men were excommunicated. As with cases of falsehood, whether rates of excommunication were deliberately or coincidentally disproportionate by gender is a matter of speculation, especially for an offense with so few examples. It may be that men, in positions of authority over their households, were held more accountable for spiritual leadership. Heyrman writes of Southern men who humored their wives' religion with a "combination of masterful indulgence and bemused condescension," as evangelical preachers attempted to gather more men into their church folds. According to Heyrman, "preserving manly independence did mean that husbands would keep their own counsel on religious matters, and that wives would refrain from challenging those views too often or too forthrightly." Perhaps in some Southern churches, as in many Southern homes,

[22] David Benedict, *A General History of the Baptist Denomination in America*, vol. 2 (Boston: Lincoln & Edmands, 1813) 113.

"women did not rank as worthy opponents in religious debate."[23]

Men who showed a willingness to reconsider their positions and be instructed by the church were retained in membership, while those who were obstinate faced excommunication. While men were charged with specific doctrinal heresies (such as universalism), only one woman faced such a charge. Instead, women received discipline most often for ecumenism (fellowshipping with other denominations); when a member chose to join the Methodists, a church was left with no alternative. Other than ecumenism, women also faced vague charges of heresy, or as in the case of the Roaring River woman, startling charges such as getting drunk and claiming that she saw Christ on the cross "with her natural eyes."

Taken as a whole, discipline cases for offenses of contention reveal a uniform standard for all church members, male and female. Church covenants were designed to maintain the unity of the whole; all members were to be in subjection to one another and to their common Master. All faced discipline for non-attendance or for leaving the church in a disorderly fashion. More women were excommunicated for telling lies and for heresy, but more men were excommunicated for general contention. In most categories, the statistics are remarkably equal. Where inequality did exist, as in cases of contention and inappropriate language, it was most often in favor of female members. The patience shown towards contentious women such as Sister Jameson and Sister Belew should not be overlooked. Contrary to much historiography, this evidence fails to suggest that church discipline enforced a double standard for men and women. Rather, it concerned the unity of the whole congregation. As will be seen in

---

[23] Christine Heyrman, *Southern Cross: The Beginnings of the Bible Belt* (Chapel Hill: University of North Carolina Press, 1997) 186–88.

the next chapter, the one major category of unbalanced discipline cases was concerned, ironically, with the subjection of men.

3

CRUCIFYING THE CARNAL MAN

Next to non-attendance, the most common type of discipline case involved excessive drinking, and the accused were almost always men. Men were also more likely than women to be disciplined for a class of offenses that could be labeled "rowdiness," which included several that were often tied to alcohol consumption, such as anger, vulgarity, violence, and unacceptable recreational activities.[1]

The way in which churches viewed drinking and drunkenness can be better understood in light of social norms of the day. Water was often unsafe to drink, and beer and other low-alcoholic drinks were popular in America from the beginning of

---

[1] According to Janet Moore Lindman, white men "bore accusations such as swearing, gaming, and drinking to excess as well as arguing with others." She goes on to state that, in spite of society's approval, churches were opposed to activities such as dancing, drinking, gaming, and attending horse races (*A World of Baptists: Gender, Race, and Religious Community in Pennsylvania and Virginia, 1689–1825* [Minneapolis: University of Minnesota, 1994] 210, 223). Spruill describes various corporal punishments colonial courts issued against women for offenses such as drinking, swearing, and fighting (*Women's Life and Work in the Southern Colonies* [Chapel Hill: University of North Carolina Press, 1938] 333–35).

European settlement. Eighteenth-century Americans drank these low-alcohol beverages frequently and in large quantities. But in spite of considerably high drinking statistics, early Americans were not generally "problem drinkers." Most drinking was family and community-oriented. And of course, churches used wine in communion services. Moderate alcohol consumption was acceptable to nearly everyone.[2]

On occasions when individuals offended community expectations, churches and civil officials both sought to restore the offender to the values of the fold. Throughout the colonies, drunkenness could be penalized with fines, imprisonment, and even corporal punishment. As noted by Mark Lender and James Martin,

> The long sermons and the stern laws did not reflect a wave of problem drinking; instead, they served to reinforce community norms, which were largely effective in restraining deviant behavior. Both civil and clerical leaders knew this and, secure in popular support, they were often sparing in applying legal and religious sanctions. As long as they could defend and demonstrate the authority of the community, and if the individual acknowledged his or her error (often as a public testament) and agreed to return to the fold, the colonials could be remarkably lenient with the occasional drunkard.[3]

Americans showed more concern with alcohol abuse when distilled beverages such as rum and whiskey gradually eclipsed the old low-alcohol favorites as the eighteenth century progressed. Some leaders feared that social norms were loosening to the point of anarchy, especially on the frontier where drunkenness came to seem rampant. As early as the 1730s, Governor Oglethorpe of Georgia banned hard liquors, but his experiment

[2] Mark Edward Lender and James Kirby Martin, *Drinking in America: A History* (London: The Free Press, 1982) 1–21.

[3] Ibid., 18.

with prohibition failed after only a few years. The famous patriot-doctor Benjamin Rush encouraged temp-erance decades later in *An Inquiry into the Effects of Ardent Spirits on the Human Body and Mind*, concerned that stability and virtue was at risk in American society.[4] But even then, very few Americans advocated total abstinence from alcoholic beverages. Quakers and Methodists were among that minority; Baptists generally were not.[5] That a church member occasionally had one too many should come as no surprise.

Churches also existed in a society where violence was accepted to a great degree. According to Bertram Wyatt-Brown, Southern society accepted violence as a natural exercise in male honor. Brown suggests that prior to the mid-eighteenth century, Southern society lived in an "Age of Custom," a time of crude living conditions, superstition, low church attendance, and brutality. It was commonplace for men to fight, for gentlemen to "duel," in pursuit of social esteem—Southern honor. It was not until the second half of the eighteenth century, he argues, that churches gained enough influence to temper the harshness of Southern society by adding piety to honor as a new Southern value. According to Elliott Gorn, even after many Southerners, especially Low Country aristocrats, abandoned the cruder forms of violence for the gentility of dueling, rough-and-tumble practices such as gouging out eyeballs survived in the backwoods regions among the lower classes.[6]

---

[4] Benjamin Rush, *Inquiry into the effects of ardent spirits on the human body and mind* (Boston: Thomas and Andrews, 1784).

[5] Lender and Martin, *Drinking in America*, 30–40.

[6] Bertram Wyatt-Brown, *The Shaping of Southern Culture: Honor, Grace, and War, 1760s–1880s* (Chapel Hill: University of North Carolina Press, 2001) 88–94. See also Elliott J. Gorn, "'Gouge and Bite, Pull Hair and Scratch': The Social Significance of Fighting in the Southern

In addition to violence, Southern churches found themselves surrounded by recreational activities such as horse racing and gambling. In the eighteenth century, horse racing was a free social event—the "sport of all" intended to feed locals "starved of organized public entertainment." Horse races contributed to community spirit and elite paternalism, but they came to be associated with the less savory activities that accompanied the races such as traveling shows, gaming booths, beer tents, cock fights, boxing and wrestling matches, and open-air dancing.[7] According to Bertram Wyatt-Brown, the society of the American South found such activities perfectly acceptable for males young and old. From their youth, Southern men experienced the permissiveness of a family and society that not only accepted but also expected such behavior from them: "Fighting, horse racing, gambling, swearing, drinking, and wenching were all activities that tested the school-boy's honor among his peers."[8] Southern society, he argues, sanctified gambling as an exercise in camaraderie and community loyalty; "betting was almost a social obligation when men gathered at barbecues, taverns, musters, supper and jockey clubs, racetracks, and on steamboats."[9]

Backcountry," *American Historical Review* 90 (February 1985): 18–43 and Wilbur Cash, *The Mind of the South* (New York: Alfred A. Knopf, 1941).

[7] Wray Vamplew, *The Turf: A Social and Economic History of Horse Racing* (London: Allen Lane, 1976) 17–18.

[8] Bertram Wyatt-Brown, *Southern Honor: Ethics and Behavior in the Old South* (New York: Oxford University Press, 1982) 164.

[9] Ibid., 343. See also T. H. Breen, "Horses and Gentlemen: The Cultural Significance of Gambling among the Gentry of Virginia," *William and Mary Quarterly*, 3d ser., 34 (April 1977); and Rhys Isaac, "Evangelical Revolt: The Nature of the Baptists' Challenge to the Traditional Order in Virginia, 1765 to 1775," *William and Mary Quarterly*, 3d ser., 31 (July 1974).

According to T. H. Breen, horse racing increasingly became the domain of the elite over the eighteenth century. The event represented the materialism, individualism, and competition that they valued so highly. And according to Nancy Struna, horse racing was for ladies as well as gentlemen in the eighteenth century. Elite coastal women not only attended but also rode in horse races and participated in the gambling that accompanied the events. Men even encouraged their participation, expecting their presence to exert a positive influence on the manners of male participants.[10] As Breen and Struna observe, Southern society said it was okay for both "gentlemen" and "ladies" to participate in horse racing and gambling. Southerners were reluctant to curb such popular activities by either mores or civil laws, but churches held members accountable to a higher standard.

Churches also condemned recreational activities such as dancing and carnal music. Methodist Bishop John Early also condemned members of his audience in North Carolina for their carnality. He "turned one out of the Society for going to a dance in public," and "cautioned the Methodists against being found in the wicked customs of the week of Christmas."[11] Although Early was constantly arguing with Baptists over their doctrinal differences, condemnation of carnality was one of the few points upon which they could agree. There is no indication in any of the Baptist church records that members celebrated customs associated with Christmas; some churches even avoided using the popular names for days of the week and months of the year,

---

[10] Breen, "Horses and Gentlemen"; Nancy Struna, "Gender and Sporting Practice in Early America, 1750–1810," *Journal of Sport History* 18/1 (Spring 1991): 10–30.

[11] John Early Diary, 1807–1814, Southern Historical Collection (Louis Round Wilson Special Collections Library, University of North Carolina, Chapel Hill NC) book 3, pp. 9–11.

presumably because of their pagan roots. They plainly denounced dancing. Charleston pastor Oliver Hart condemned dancing in a sermon entitled "Dancing Exploded, A sermon shewing the unlawfulness, sinfulness, and bad consequences of balls, assemblies, and dances in general."[12] Article 7 of the Mechanicsville Church Covenant condemned such behavior in no uncertain terms, listing "dancing, horseracing, card playing, dice, billiards, and the wanton, profligate manner in which many spend the Lord's day" as activities Christians should avoid.

Lindman suggests that there was a culture clash between evangelicals and Southern society, which expected men to be hard drinkers, fighters, and gamblers. Both she and Heyrman argue that Southern evangelical men consciously toughened up their image to gain the respect of their society, in turn influencing the Southern ideal of masculinity.[13] Church records provide evidence that such a clash of cultures did indeed exist. These churches made a serious effort to civilize the manners of their members, if not the society in which they lived. Southern churches viewed intoxication, violence, and gambling on horse races as transgressions against the subjection they demanded of godly men and women.

In keeping with tradition, churches used wine in their observance of the Lord's Supper. And along with most of their society, they also believed that casual drinking was acceptable in moderation. Skewarkey articulated its position in a 1794 query: "How far shall a person proceed in drinking spiritous liquors before he can be said to be drunk therewith[?].... We think when

[12] Pamphlet by Oliver Hart, "Dancing Exploded, A sermon shewing the unlawfulness, sinfulness, and bad consequences of balls, assemblies, and dances in general" (Charleston: David Bruce, 1778).

[13] Janet Moore Lindman, "Acting the Manly Christian: White Evangelical Masculinity in Revolutionary Virginia," *William and Mary Quarterly* 57 (April 2000).

a person partakes of so much spiritous liquor as to disorder mind or body, that he is guilty of intemperance and consequently sins in such proceedings." Article 10 of the Mechanicsville Covenant stated,

> As the drinking of intoxicating liquors to excess is a prevalent vice of the age in which we live, and has often ruined the reputation of christians [*sic*], we therefore resolve that if we use them at all it shall be in moderation and as we conscientiously believe they may be innocently received in the sight of God.

While most church members appear to have known when to put down the bottle, as other members of society, occasionally one would go beyond the acceptable point.

A few interesting patterns emerge from a systematic survey of drunkenness cases. There were more drunkenness charges during the spring and autumn months. These seasons correspond with planting and harvesting. Poor farmers would have been more likely to have money in their pockets and would have attended community events such as workings and parties at such times. Although statistics varied among regions and churches, on average a church disciplined one member for drunkenness every year or two, and approximately one-third of those cases ended in excommunication. The offending member was usually male. He sometimes made a voluntary confession and sometimes answered a charge made by a fellow member, either male or female. In most cases, he would have been suspended for a short period and restored to fellowship after acknowledging his fault and showing evidence of proper repentance. This gender-specific category of church discipline shows that in the moral economy of these churches, men too were to be "in subjection" to the church and to God.

SEASONAL DRUNKENNESS PATTERNS

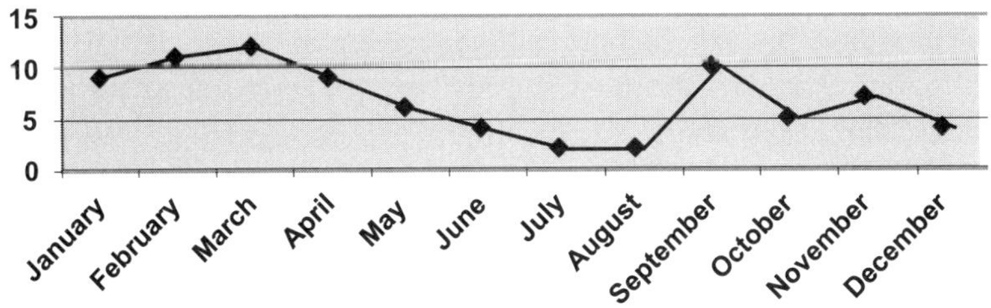

Drunkenness charges of Clear Springs, Reedy River, Tyger, Skewarkey, Brier Creek, and Welsh Neck

Geographical patterns are also evident. Several historians have studied the elevated rates of intoxication and violence in Up Country regions. Some have pointed to ethnicity as an explanation, suggesting, for example, that men of Scots-Irish ancestry were particularly prone to heavy drinking and hard fighting. Although culture likely did have an influence, culture alone fails to explain the tendencies of such a diverse region. Other historians have examined the subject through the lens of honor and community instability. On the fringe of civilization, the Up Country was plagued by poverty, disease, warfare, and weak institutional structures. A clear example is the Regulator Movement in South Carolina, in which vigilantes frustrated with rampant crime and ineffective legal institutions took the law into their own hands.[14] Not all violence was sparked by alcohol, but drinking often fanned the flames.

---

[14] Thomas P. Slaughter, *The Whiskey Rebellion: Frontier Epilogue to the American Revolution* (New York: Oxford University Press, 1986); Dickson D. Bruce, Jr., *Violence and Culture in the Antebellum South*

Widespread landlessness added significantly to the frustration of Up Country inhabitants. Land claims were often disputed and lost, and much of the best land was taken up by speculators by the second half of the eighteenth century. This economic reality, more than any other factor, fueled habitual migration. Poor farmers dreaming of a piece of land to call their own often followed that dream deeper and deeper into the wilderness of hopes deferred. Repeated failure no doubt contributed to great frustration and anxiety, especially for men whose honor depended upon their ability to provide for their families. In a culture where alcohol was available and acceptable, it is not surprising that many men turned to the bottle as a way of coping with anxiety.[15] Furthermore, considering farmers' wounded sense of honor, it seems natural that intoxication was often paired with violent assertions of manliness.

Low Country South Carolina was one of the first regions in the American South to be settled by the English. As early as the late seventeenth century, "Charles Town" was emerging as a center of culture and trade. This area was home to the First Baptist Church of Charleston and the nearby Ashley River and was the center of the Charleston Baptist Association, the second in America. To the north, the Cheraws District (later Darlington County) lay along the Pee Dee River. It was in the area of Society Hill (near Darlington) that Welsh Baptists from Pennsylvania settled after receiving royal land grants in the 1730s. The Welshmen raised flax, hemp, and other agricultural goods, retaining much cultural hegemony until many immigrants of other backgrounds began arriving later in the century. Low

---

(Austin: University of Texas Press, 1979). David Hackett Fischer, *Albion's Seed: Four British Folkways in America* (New York: Oxford University Press, 1989); Gorn, "Gouge and Bite."

[15] W. J. Rorabaugh, *The Alcoholic Republic, an American Tradition* (New York: Oxford University Press, 1979).

Country South Carolina was one of the most stable areas of Colonial America and was also among the most prosperous, as evidenced by the extent of slaveholding and trade.

Church record books from Low Country South Carolina show that members did come under discipline for drunkenness, but at a rate lower than that of the rest of the Carolinas. Here churches dealt with a case of drunkenness once every four years on average. Drunkenness was also less likely to be accompanied by violence in this region. By the early nineteenth century, drunkenness cases became increasingly rare. It is likely that relative social and economic stability mitigated the rate of drunkenness, but it certainly did not eliminate it altogether. More prosperous Southerners may have drunk different intoxicants, for different reasons, in different amounts, or in a different context than their poorer neighbors. They may have become intoxicated less than others, but it is also possible that drunkenness was a private affair their society was more willing to overlook than the public disorder of less-prestigious drinkers. The Welsh Neck records reveal that men censured for intoxication could expect a great deal of patience with their faults. Even when an offender remained obstinate, the church was sometimes reluctant to make a public scene over his excommunication. In 1765, the church agreed to abandon the practice of public announcements of church discipline for private suspension instead.

Up Country church records from both the Carolinas contain more references to drunkenness and violence than for Low Country South Carolina. A wave of migrants, primarily from Pennsylvania, settled along the eastern edge of the Blue Ridge Mountains from the 1760s onwards. Baptist churches, just as the migrants, appeared first along the Yadkin River in North Carolina, and later in Greenville County, South Carolina, toward the end of the century. A large proportion of this migration was German and Scots-Irish.[16] Methodist Bishop Early wrote of the prevalence of drunkenness in the journals he kept of his travels in North Carolina. When he visited Flatty Creek Chapel during his 1808 Camden Circuit, he observed, "We had meeting that night and I believe great good would have been done if we had not been molested by a drunkard who came there drunk. (I have had six meetings there and every other time a drunkard has molested us. Here drunken magistrates make drunken subjects. Oh Lord, alarm the swine before they plunge into eternal ruin.)" And while visiting Concord, South Carolina, on his Greenville Circuit of 1811–1812, he wrote, "There I understand that nearly the whole society of men would take too much of Dutch courage, brandy or wines, and I determined to break up the practice or expel them from connection."[17] He likely had his hands full. Why might drunkenness have been more prevalent in some areas than others? Church and civil records both suggest that this area fit the Up Country model of poverty and instability. Frequent dismissals of relocating church members suggest economic failure. In addition to relocation, other indicators of a region's relative wealth are the rate of slave ownership and taxation.

Church membership lists and business proceedings show that slave ownership was not as widespread west of the Fall Line, and census records attest as well to the disparity of slavery in the east and west. Slaves made up approximately 30 percent

---

[16] Native Americans scornfully referred to the new immigrants as "Virginians." See Tom Hatley, *The Dividing Paths: Cherokees and South Carolinians through the Revolutionary Era* (New York: Oxford University Press, 1995).

[17] John Early Diary, 1807–1814, Southern Historical Collection (Louis Round Wilson Special Collections Library, University of North Carolina, Chapel Hill NC) book 3, p. 2; book 7, p. 174.

of the population in both the Cheraw District of South Carolina and Martin County, North Carolina. To the west, however, slaves made up only 10 percent of the population in Greenville, South Carolina, and 7 percent in Wilkes County, North Carolina.[18]

Census Statistics (Federal Census of 1790)

County/District	Total	Slaves	Percentage
Greenville, SC	6508	606	9.3
Wilkes, NC	8156	549	6.7
Cheraw, SC	10706	3200	29.9
Martin, NC	6080	1889	31

Tax lists also offer insight into the economic state of counties and individual inhabitants. Unfortunately, tax lists surviving from this time are rare. Many such records have been destroyed by fire and negligence, but the ones that remain yield useful clues. The Wilkes County, North Carolina, tax list for 1782 reports a total county assessment of £77,710. In 1805, the average land holding was 186 acres per poll, and in both years (1782 and 1805) more than 200 household heads were landless. To the east, Martin County, North Carolina, was assessed in 1779 for more than £1 million.[19]

One might expect Low Country North Carolina to resemble Low Country South Carolina more closely than the Up Country, but such was not always the case. An unusually detailed record book has survived to tell the story of the Skewarkey church. Skewarkey was located in the area of Tar Landing along the Roanoke River in Martin County. Skewarkey belonged to the Kehukee Baptist Association, the fourth in America. Records for

[18] 1790 Census, North Carolina State Archives, Raleigh NC.

[19] Wilkes County NC tax lists 1782, 1805; Martin County NC tax list 1779. North Carolina State Archives, Raleigh NC.

Skewarkey and other churches in this region date back to the 1770s and 80s, contemporaneous with those in Up Country North Carolina. Discipline statistics suggest that this region was as much of a problem area in terms of drunkenness and violence as the Up Country. This appears to be a puzzling exception at first glance; closer examination confirms that the instability model may apply here as well, but in combination with other factors.

When church record books are considered individually, it becomes apparent that cases of drunkenness and violence were common in Skewarkey and Sandy Creek, but not in Sandy Run or Poplar Spring. It has already been established that the region was relatively stable economically, since tax assessments and rates of slave ownership were considerably higher than western counties. What, then, was going on in churches such as Skewarkey that appear to have experienced economic hardship? Clues are to be found upon comparing the 1786 church membership list with civil records such as the census, tax lists, and land grants.

According to the 1790 census, a few church members owned small numbers of slaves, and several owned none. Seven identifiable men owned between one and three slaves each, and five owned none. Jesse Pierce is listed as owning nine slaves. The names of three men are listed twice, so it is uncertain from the census whether Martin Ross of Skewarkey owned twelve or none, John Bennett 11 or none, and William Hyman 5 or none. That slavery was present in the church is also confirmed by occasional references to "servants" in church records. There is physical evidence, as well, in the slave gallery in the meeting house built in the mid-nineteenth century.[20]

---

[20] 1790 Census, Martin County NC. North Carolina State Archives, Raleigh NC.

Church members included in the 1779 Martin County tax list were assessed at an average of approximately £1,000. Interestingly, both Jesse Pierce and Benjamin Blount, who would later be dependent upon the church's financial assistance, fell into this range. Only one, Edward Byrd, was taxed significantly higher at more than £6,000. Interestingly, Byrd was among the repeat offenders for drunkenness. Byrd faced charges in 1790 and again in 1805 but remained in church fellowship. The other three repeat offenders were all excommunicated: William Cane after four offenses, Edmund Smithwick after three, and Abraham Chappell after two. Later in the history of Skewarkey Baptist Church, four men were excommunicated for drunkenness after only one offense. Of those four, only Anthony Burroughs (whose charges also included unpaid debt and attempted suicide) is listed in the 1790 census. Two others of the last name Duggan may have been sons of Duggans who were listed in the 1790 census. These scattered clues suggest that men excommunicated for drunkenness were more likely to be "newcomers" or otherwise without social status. The only one listed in the 1790 census, Anthony Burroughs, was clearly a financial failure. Others may have been younger sons and newcomers to the region who had more difficulty establishing themselves financially.

Skewarkey Taxpayers (Martin County Tax List of 1779)

Name	*£*	*S*	*cts.*
Kader Biggs	416	15	2
James Biggs	349	14	0
Joseph Biggs	1085	0	0
William Biggs	443	14	0
Jacob Tice	1120	10	0
Edward Byrd	6349	0	0
John Ward	820	6	0

Benjamin Blount	1140	11	7
William Hyman	1631	17	6
Jesse Pierce	1085	0	0
Hardy Stallings	1000	12	0

Average: approximately £1400

Average (excluding Byrd): approximately £900

Joseph and William Biggs, among Skewarkey's original members, held several land grants. Interestingly, the Biggs family was involved in multiple lawsuits and land disputes that came under the church's consideration.[21] In 1790, William was excommunicated for initiating a lawsuit, as executor of an estate, against some of the brethren without the church's permission. He was readmitted, however, and in 1810 he was named as executor to James Collins, who left part of his estate to the church.[22] Another member of the Biggs family, Kedar, was likely cautioned by William's example when he asked for the church's permission before pursuing legal steps against fellow members as executor of an estate.

In 1805, William Biggs was involved in a land dispute with Brothers Nowell and Harrell. The church appears to have sided with Biggs in its arbitration, for the other two men and one of their wives were afterward excommunicated for not abiding by an agreement formerly made between them. The Biggs family was not the only leading family to be involved in such cases. In 1792, the church also arbitrated a land dispute between Edward Byrd and Jess Pierce. Judging from Jess's slaves and Byrd's tax assessment, the two men were among the wealthiest members of

[21] See ch. 4 for a detailed discussion of these cases. See also land grants records in North Carolina State Archives, Raleigh NC.

[22] James Collins is said to have been a black man. See Francis Manning and W.H. Booker, *Religion and Education in Martin County 1774–1974* (Williamston NC: Enterprise Publishing Company, 1974) 71.

the church. Others involved in land disputes left a lesser imprint in the historical record. Perhaps some of them fell into the category of the disadvantaged newcomers, but in the absence of direct links between poverty and members involved in drunkenness cases, it is impossible to be sure of the influence financial circumstances had on the behavior of individual members. Ideological factors should also be taken into consideration.

Clearly, not all members of churches such as Skewarkey were living in poverty. Some possessed land, several slaves, and a sufficient income. It is probable that newcomers to the region found it more difficult to become comfortably settled than the older inhabitants did. But other factors related to a church's income should not be overlooked. Skewarkey's small membership must have limited its resources, even though several of its members were situated comfortably. Ideology, then, is also a factor. When churches such as Skewarkey held to doctrine and practice that effectively "purged" the church of offending members through excommunication, strict discipline was sure to reduce membership lists as well as tithes. Consideration of personal agency, then, must be added to economic circumstances in order to understand disproportionate rates of disciplinary action between different churches. Economic variables likely influenced the behavior of individual members, but a church's moral economy also influenced its own economic situation. Although the membership in general was not poor, the church was. Its strict discipline for drunkenness and other offenses kept the membership small and the finances limited.

Slavery seemed to have a lesser presence in Skewarkey than in the church's region as a whole. The church records themselves contain evidence concerning the rate of slave ownership. The Skewarkey membership list of the 1780s shows no indication that any slaves were church members at that time. There are however occasional references to slaves in discipline cases, one in 1793 and three in 1804–1805. Minutes also make occasional reference to the baptism of a slave, but such is also the case for Up Country churches. Sandy Creek does not appear to have had any slaves on its earlier membership list, but ten "persons of color" do appear on the 1818 list. Sandy Run, on the other hand, had an extensive list of slaves and a separate list dividing white members and free persons of color. There is mention in the records of separate services for "Negroes" in 1799, and the church's biographical sketch of its late pastor Lemuel Burkitt referred to him as an "indulgent master." Poplar Spring's membership lists do not mention slaves, but the records make frequent mention of "servants."

The presence of slavery is not the only indicator of wealth to be found in church records. Skewarkey's detailed records of church business make it clear that money was in short supply for the church. The church often paid its pastor in produce, livestock, and articles of clothing, and members tithed in corn and pork as well. Male members maintained the meeting house and grounds themselves, and members in need were provided not with money but with produce and services such as splitting firewood. Several members were exempted from making certain contributions to the church due to their dire need although a query of 1795 stated that no member was too poor to contribute something as a mandatory tithe. It is likely that poverty among members strained the church's resources, given the frequent inquiries whether members qualified as "poor of the church" and the controversial 1812 query about the duty to relieve such members.

Skewarkey's economic circumstances likely had much to do with the frequent dismissal of relocating members, especially after 1805. Turkey Creek also witnessed a mass migration of couples to Kentucky in the 1790s. Discipline cases involving land disputes and debt are common features in church record books from every region except for Low Country South Carolina. As did Up Country churches, Skewarkey dealt with cases involving land disputes, broken contracts, lawsuits, covetousness, and theft. It is also likely that many vague discipline cases of contention between members featured economic roots.[23]

Lower rates of cases involving drunkenness and violence in Low Country South Carolina churches may have been due in part to economic prosperity. In Low Country South Carolina, Welsh Neck suspended eleven male members for drunkenness in the 1760s. Ashley River suspended five between 1740 and 1752. Cashaway also disciplined members for drunkenness. Such cases, however, dwindled over the second half of the eighteenth century. Either fewer members were getting drunk, or churches lost the will to expose such offenses at the expense of their membership lists and financial resources. Most likely, both were partially true. With the region's increased stability came a decrease in pressures that often led men to drink. Furthermore, the rise of respectability among churches and individuals and privacy would have likely tempted churches to turn a blind eye to the bad habits of the most prominent members.

Drunkenness among the clergy stood out from the typical procedure of suspension and restoration. In the 1760s, Cashaway took up the case of minister Joshua Edwards, who confessed to drunkenness. The church suspended him from the ministry and from communion privileges and asked neighboring Welsh Neck for further advice in the case. Welsh Neck removed a deacon from office in 1760 for drunkenness. Ashley River admonished its pastor, John Stephens, for drunkenness in August 1768 and removed him from office the following January.

Churches from outside the region occasionally excommunicated a minister in a drunkenness case. In May 1821, William Ferrington acknowledged before Brier Creek that he was guilty

[23] See ch. 4 for a more detailed discussion of Skewarkey's finances.

of drunkenness. The church restored him to fellowship but barred him from "exercising his gift" until the church granted permission to resume preaching. The very next month, he asked for permission but was denied. He then displayed a "hard spirit" against the church, insisted on preaching anyway, and was promptly excommunicated for his obstinacy. Eaton's excommunicated a black man (who was licensed to preach in 1806) for drunkenness, disobedience to his master, lying, and theft. Even pastors, then, were to be in subjection, especially since they were expected to set a positive example for other men to follow.

Of the four regions studied here, Up Country North Carolina was the strictest in its dealings with intemperance. In addition to the preacher it excommunicated in 1821, Brier Creek excommunicated four other male members for persistent intoxication between 1793 and 1821. Five men were forgiven and retained in fellowship during the same period upon acknowledging their fault, one of them a repeat offender. One man was excommunicated after a year of suspension, repeated offenses, and denial. Another simply failed to appear at the church meeting when cited, and was promptly excommunicated. One man was excommunicated within a month after acknowledging his fault but failing to give satisfaction that he had changed his behavior. Another did come but failed to give the church satisfaction, "appeared very stubborn," and was censured until three months later, when he again "refused to give satisfaction or answer fair questions" and was excommunicated.[24]

Brier Creek's 50 percent excommunication rate for drinking offenses was higher than the average for North and South Carolina yet lower than that of its region in Up Country North Carolina. Jersey excommunicated all five of its offenders

---

[24] Brier Creek, 1793–1794, 1802, 1820, 1806.

between 1788 and 1810, but several of these cases were linked to other offenses. One man was charged in November 1792 with drinking too much and abusing his wife. He appeared on his second citation, acknowledged his transgression, and then repeatedly requested patience. The church's patience wore out in February 1794, and he was finally excommunicated. In 1799, another man was quickly excommunicated for drinking, swearing, stabbing his brother, and "other ill behavior." One man was forgiven in 1806 but then excommunicated for his second offense a few months later. In addition to excommunicating a black preacher in 1806, Eaton's also excommunicated two men in 1801 for drunkenness, compounded with nonattendance, profane language, and refusing to obey the church's authority. No man disciplined for drunkenness in Jersey or Eaton's was retained in fellowship after a period of suspension. Roaring River had a lower excommunication rate. Two men were excommunicated for drunkenness in 1786 and 1788, and five continued in church fellowship after acknowledging their offense and making recantation in 1788 and 1792. Of the two women accused of drunkenness, one was restored in 1793. The other, whose case was complicated with a charge of heresy, was excommunicated in 1797.

David Benedict noted that churches in the Broad River Association of Up Country South Carolina gained many members during revivals at the turn of the century, but many of those new members soon moved to the west or were excommunicated. Between 1803 and 1808, area churches excommunicated 285 members, according to Benedict, "which circumstance proves that they received much chaff with the precious grain, as is too often the case in such great ingatherings; it also proves that they have used a commendable degree of diligence in winnowing it out, when it was discovered."[25] It is likely that many of those had consumed too much "precious grain" of another sort!

Drunkenness cases are too plentiful and uniform to describe in detail; a few cases, however, stand out from the rest. A man of Bear Creek was actually drunk at a church conference in 1795. Another man was able to give the church satisfaction regarding his operating a tavern that same year, but the church was not satisfied when it excommunicated him for drunkenness in 1798. Yadkin was "grieved" in 1789 when a man of the church was charged with "carrying of liquor [to] a place of Election…treating the people [to free drinks, presumably to buy votes]." The church referred the case in a query to the next association meeting, where it was agreed that such conduct was not lawful.

Most of the offenders were white men, but when a black man of Poplar Spring was accused in 1793 of stealing and drinking brandy, he gave satisfaction and was restored two months later. A Reedy River woman acknowledged she had drunk too much liquor and was restored in October 1814. And in 1801, Tyger considered a report that a married couple had been "over taken in liquor." The church bore with them, even when the man repeated the offense twice in the following months and requested forgiveness. In 1809, the same church censured a woman for being drunk and restored her upon her recantation. Bush River also dealt with a woman for drunkenness in 1805. Turkey Creek censured a woman for drunkenness in 1812 but restored her to fellowship. A Lick Fork woman also confessed to drunkenness in 1795. In 1816, that church excommunicated a female slave for the same offense. Just as the men, women who were guilty of drunkenness could expect to find forgiveness

---

[25] David Benedict, *A General History of the Baptist Denomination in America*, vol. 2 (Boston: Lincoln & Edmands, 1813) 159.

upon acknowledgment and repentance of their offense, but those who refused to confess or forsake their sin were excommunicated.

Drunkenness charges were often tied to discipline cases involving other offenses such as angry "passion," inappropriate language, and violence.[26] As seen in chapter two, women and men were both often charged with bickering and backbiting. Women were also occasionally seen displaying violent tempers and vulgar language, but not as often as men. Sandy Creek suspended a woman in 1773 for quarreling, swearing, and threatening to beat another woman (apparently a relative) with knives. Roaring River excommunicated a husband and wife in 1794, the man for charging another man to fight, and the woman for threatening to kill another woman. Wheeley's demanded satisfaction of a couple in 1795, the wife for beating another woman, and the husband for "approbating her conduct." But men faced such charges much more often than women. Welsh Neck suspended several male members for offenses such as profanity, rash speech, lying, and (in one case) beating a neighbor. Cashaway routinely dealt with members for inappropriate language and demeanor, and Ashley River for ill words and disorderly conduct.[27] Churches outside Low Country South Carolina also suspended members for similar offenses: being "in a passion," swearing, lying, and taking God's name in vain. Those offences were fairly uniform across regions, but, as discussed earlier, violence appears to have been more widespread outside Low Country South Carolina, and more so

[26] See, for example, Shoal Creek 1796, Lick Fork 1808, Turkey Creek 1808, Bush River 1805–1806. Fighting was also accompanied often by participation in shoots and other sorts of "gaming." See Bush River 1804–1805.

[27] See Welsh Neck, Cashaway, and Ashley River 1760s.

in certain churches where poverty and drunkenness were also prominent.

One such church was Reedy River. A man made recantation there in 1801 for "striking a lad for (as he thought) some bad conduct, in killing his hogs" and was forgiven. In 1804, a man was excommunicated for drinking too much and "striping to fight." In 1806 a man acknowledged he had "been out of the way by passion and offering to fight," and the church bore with him. In 1818, a man got "in a passion" so much that he whipped his daughter-in-law. He acknowledged his crime and gave "satisfaction" to the church that he had repented. The records are similar for Tyger. In 1804, a man confessed he was wrong to hit his brother in a fight. Another man who was accused of whipping his wife failed to convince the church he was justified in doing so. In 1806 a man acknowledged getting angry, quarrelling, pulling off his clothes and offering to fight. His repentance satisfied the church. In 1808 a man was accused of "being overtaken in passion" and "collering" another man. He also gave the church satisfaction of repentance. In 1810 a man confessed that he had gotten angry and raised a gun at another man "in way of defence and told him not to raise his or else." And in 1811 a man "rose up on account of an unfellowship with himself for wrangling" with another man. Part of the church was satisfied after "long dealing" with him. As these cases illustrate, churches were willing to forgive acts of violence, but not to overlook them, whether men abused other men, women, or children.

Other churches had a higher excommunication rate for cases involving violence. But in all churches, excommunication or restoration seems to have depended upon whether the offender showed repentance. A Jersey man accused of getting drunk and abusing his wife was eventually excommunicated. In 1799 a man was excommunicated for stabbing his brother, along with drinking, swearing, and "other ill behavior." Brier Creek excommunicated a man in 1792 for "getting mad and wanting to fight." And in 1799 a man was excommunicated for getting angry, wanting to fight, and failing to appear when cited. Roaring River In 1791 Poplar Spring excommunicated a man for "justifying himself" in wickedness and fighting, and the following year it excommunicated another man for fighting, excess drinking, and dancing. Bush River excommunicated a man in 1802 for beating his brother. When a man of Turkey Creek in 1811 was charged with being "drunk at muster and riding after a man saying he would whip him," he refused to give the church satisfaction for his behavior. A Shoal Creek man, on the other hand, does not appear to have been excommunicated when he confessed to striking another man with a switch in 1776.

Several men disciplined for violence were repeat offenders. Such was the case with the Maners of Roaring River. In 1790 Gibson Maner accused Christopher Maner of "striping to fight." Christopher repented, but the following year he was once again brought under church discipline for violence. He admitted that he had threatened to kill a man but refused to repent, insisting that "he should do it if it was to doe again." In 1793, Gibson Maner (Christopher's accuser) made recantation for getting angry and fighting.[28]

---

[28] Christopher may have been Gibson's son, although their relationship is uncertain. Gibson Maner is found in the Wilkes County census of 1800 to have had one male under the age of sixteen living in his household, along with seven females and no slaves. He acquired a land grant of fifty acres in the 1790s. And in a tax list for the year 1784, Gibson is reported to have had 150 acres of land. Christopher, although he is counted as a poll, has no land of his own. See Wilkes County land grants, 1784 tax list, and 1800 census. See North Carolina Land Grants, Tax Lists, and Census in the North Carolina State Archives, Raleigh NC.

Skewarkey had an especially high rate of discipline cases involving violence, often describing unjustified fighting with the phrase "fist of wickedness." In 1788 a man was charged with "behaving in a disagreeable manner in offering to smite with the fist of wickedness." A man was excommunicated for getting drunk and fighting in 1803, and the next year another man was also charged with drinking and offering to smite with the fist of wickedness. In 1805 a man was excommunicated for the fist of wickedness, in addition to dishonest trade and false testimony. In 1808 a man was charged with drinking and offering to fight; three months later he was excommunicated. In 1809 a black man was excommunicated for his long absence and "smiting with the fist of wickedness."

Those charged with fighting with other men were most likely to receive forgiveness. In 1821 a Brier Creek man informed the church that one of his male slaves had gotten angry with a fellow slave and that the two had "passed blows." The accused slave confessed his fault and was forgiven. Eaton's also restored a man who confessed to fighting in 1776. In 1807 Skewarkey cited a black man but then excused him for fighting on a Sunday. In 1792 Skewarkey charged a white man with "quareling with another man and spiting in his face and saying if he was able he would fight him." Upon further investigation, the church learned that he had been insulted by the other man's "abuse" of his wife. Considering it a "very trying case," the church retained both the man and his wife after admonishing them for "not behaving in a Christian like manner." But the following year the same man was excommunicated for fighting, swearing, and failing to appear.

Churches did not only disapprove of violence towards others; members were also expected to treat their own bodies, the "temple of the Lord," with respect. In 1805 Skewarkey cited a man for, in addition to a charge of non-payment, "attempting to destroy his own existance." The majority voted to continue him in fellowship at that time, but a few months later the church excommunicated him by a large majority for persistent drunkenness and failure to attend. Whether a man inflicted violence on others or himself, the church as a whole was "wounded" when a member was not in subjection to its standards of behavior. This man's case serves as a vivid example of the often-linked problems of poverty, drunkenness, and violence.

If these churches had access to the contemporary writings of William Cowper, the great poet of English evangelicalism, they would have no doubt appreciated what he had to say about carnality. He began a poem titled "The Mahometan Hog: A Tale" (later titled "The Love of the World Reproved; or, Hypocrisy Detected") by satirizing Muslims. When Mohammed commanded them to abstain from eating pork because one particular part of the pig was an abomination, they eagerly set about to find which pieces of pork meat they could safely eat and which one they must avoid. Later in the same poem, Cowper then turned his satire on Christian readers:

> "Renounce the WORLD!" the preacher cries:
> "We do," a multitude replies:
> While one as innocent regards
> A snug and friendly game at *cards*;
> And one, whatever you may say,
> Can see no evil in a *play*:
> Some love a *concert*, or a *race*;
> And others *shooting*, and the *chace*.
> Revil'd and lov'd, renounc'd and follow'd,
> Thus bit by bit the *world* is *swallow'd*:
> Each thinks his neighbour makes too free,
> Yet likes a *slice* as well as he:

With *sophistry* their sauce they sweeten,
Till quite from *tail* to *snout* 'tis eaten.[29]

Backsliding church members were often reproved for nibbling away at the world's forbidden fruit. In 1809, Tyger answered a query whether members could frequent public places of rendezvous "such as dancing schools and the like houses." The church answered that it "was not in the least tolerated, neither was it tolerated for such to keep or suffer to be kept about their houses such instrument of musick as a fiddle."[30] In order to understand why churches of this period condemned dancing and fiddle tunes, it is necessary to examine the historical context of such activities. What might they have found offensive? Arthur Hudson, in *Songs of the Carolina Charter Colonists*, describes the popular folk songs of the day, many of which were of English and Scottish origin.[31] Themes such as violence, crime, murder, betrayal, and witchcraft made up the content of a large portion of the ballads identified by Francis

[29] William Cowper, "The Mahometan Hog: A Tale," *The Gentleman's Magazine* (September 1780).

[30] "Are professors of religion, whose children live with them as members of their families, justifiable in allowing or even suffering them to go to dances, or associating with those who delight in that evil practice and its concomitants? Answer: Let parents under such circumstances not forget the case of old Eli (1 Samuel), nor the express word of God elsewhere; that children should be trained up in the way they should go, and brought up in the admonition of the Lord; for we think it inconsistent with their religious professions to indulge their children in that which they cannot allow them to participate," Kehukee Association 1799, cited in C. B. Hassell and S. Hassell, *History of the Church of God* (1886; repr., Ellenwood GA: Old School Hymnal Co., 1983) 833.

[31] Arthur Palmer Hudson, *Songs of the Carolina Charter Colonists, 1663–1763* (Raleigh: Carolina Charter Tercentenary Commission, 1962) introduction and ch. 6.

Child, themes which churches would understandably have seen as a cause for concern.

In chapter 6 of Hudson's *Songs of the Carolina Charter Colonists,* the author cites Joan Moser, who suggests that many English folk tunes and dances "hark back to ancient times when dance was an integral part of religious rituals, and the melodies and figures reflect this inheritance, surviving also in children's singing games." Moser cites Cecil Sharp to verify her observation that the American square dance,

> no longer to be found in England, is an example of an earlier and almost extinct type containing indubitably ancient figures which had their beginnings in sacrificial pagan worship ceremonies. These figures, still danced today, such as the Figure-eight, Birdie in the Cage, Wind Up the Ball of Yarn, and The Wild Goose Chase, are typical of such ancient lineage.

If churches associated popular song and dance of the day with paganism, it is not surprising that they frowned upon it. Carnality alone was offensive enough without being compounded by pagan connections.

Churches expected members, male or female, to abstain from carnality. Welsh Neck suspended a man in 1761 for getting drunk and attempting to dance in public. Brier Creek excommunicated a man in 1791 for singing carnal songs, dancing, racing, and "other carnal ways." Poplar Spring excommunicated a man in 1791 for the "sin of dancing," and the following year a man was excommunicated for dancing along with excess drinking and fighting. A Roaring River man repented in 1787 of "going to a weding." His puzzling confession makes one wonder if the festivities that often accompanied marriage ceremonies violated the church's standards of sobriety. Another man of that church made recantation the same year for "suffering dancing in his house."

Lick Fork censured a man in 1794 for dancing at a wedding, and Brushy Creek in 1801 for having a dancing school in his home. As late as 1847, Brushy Creek censured homes that harbored the fiddle and dance. Bear Creek disciplined one man for "alowing the fidle to be plade in his hous and for riot in a publick cumpany" in 1797, and excommunicated another in 1800 for allowing "frollicking in his house." Another man was censured in 1801 for "sufering danceing in his house." Gum Branch even objected when a male member in 1796 simply helped another man tune a fiddle. The brother was charged with "tuneing a fiddle for others to play." He denied the charge but admitted that he "turned one screw to make it past, so that it might hold the string tight." For this, and the additional offense of selling the fiddle on the Lord's day, he was censured.

Churches also disciplined women for dancing and other types of carnality. A woman of Wheeley's was accused in 1792 of "disorderly living such as running, jesting, joking, etc." A man of the same church repented of "reporting among the people of the world that he heard [a female member] singing a wicked or carnal song." Had it not been a false report, the church no doubt would have held the sister accountable. Lick Fork censured a woman for frequenting "frollicks" and plays in 1794. Turkey Creek also demanded satisfaction from a woman in 1802 "for the report that was going about her dancing." Although amends were made, she then requested a letter of dismissal, perhaps embarrassed by the charge. In 1811, upon hearing a report that Nancy Robartson "had been at a race and a dance," the church cited her and sent brethren to speak with her and her husband about "her having liberty to come to next meeting," at which time she gave satisfaction for her behavior. Then in 1812, the church entered into a discussion concerning the "sisters not attending meetings of business; and attending of [military] musters." A dance, then, was not the only place considered inappropriate for a lady of the church.

In 1811 Skewarkey considered an inquiry whether the church could "excuse a member who is master of a family that suffers dancing in his house, also playing cards." The church answered in the negative and proceeded to cite a man for suffering dancing and cards in his house and to excommunicate a woman for frequent dancing. The man acknowledged the charge against him and was forgiven. Perhaps men shouldered more responsibility for keeping an orderly house because of their position as heads of households or because society's expectations allowed them greater opportunity to pursue such indulgences in public. But mothers were also held accountable for the behavior of their children. Brother Northcut of Turkey Creek raised a query in 1801, asking "how far a maried woman['s] authority extends in prohibiting a daughter from going to places of carnal rendesvous." The church answered that she should "pointedly forbid them from going." Brother Northcut then suggested that the church examine Sister Posey "for keeping a disorderly house." Sister Posey was restored to fellowship, but not without reproof for her negligence. In 1806, Brother Northcut again raised a query that was almost identical to the first, asking "how far does a married woman's authority extend in forbiding her daughter from frolics where her husband does not interfere." The answer was the same: she should pointedly forbid such behavior. The church then proceeded to examine two sisters of the church "about their daughters going to dances."[32]

Men were much more likely than women to be disciplined for participating in horse races, shooting matches, and any type of gambling activity.[33] Cashaway condemned horse races and

[32] It might appear that Brother Northcut was prejudiced against female members, but he was also often seen examining male members for their offenses.

[33] "Is it thought proper to retain in fellowship a member who clears out race-paths, or suffers it to be done on his land, or who erects five batteries? Answer: No" (Kehukee Baptist Association 1823, cited in

shoots in article eight of its covenant, as its successor Mechanicsville did years later. In 1761 Welsh Neck suspended a woman for selling liquor at a horse race, and a man for being drunk at a horse race. Ashley River censured public horse races in 1746. Wheeley's censured participation in shooting matches, as well as "throwing the shoulder stone" in 1791. In 1795, it censured a man for keeping "bad company" and participating at the "five battery." A Reedy River man made a recantation in 1804 for "having a hand in a shooting match," and in 1806 a man informed the church "of his working on some race paths at [my] son's." The record reads that the behavior "hurt the men of the church very sorely. But after much deliberation and his acknowledgment satisfaction was obtained and he restored to fellowship." A Flat River query of 1786 stated that masters were not to allow their servants or children to attend cockfights, races, or dances. Lick Fork dealt with a man in 1792 for keeping drunken company in his house and shooting for brandy. Bush River condemned shooting for a prize in 1804, and in 1806 it raised an association query denouncing lottery tickets. In 1807 a Tyger man "acknowledged his fault in being too forward in encouraging beting" and was forgiven. Bear Creek cited a man in 1797 for allowing "show men to show the slight of hand in his house." A Roaring River man repented of going to a shooting match in 1787. In 1791, John Sparks and Gibson Maner repented of "gameing." Not only did the church forgive the men, but it also delegated them to represent the church at the next association meeting. Two years later, however, Maner was again reproved for his participation in a shooting match. Skewarkey

---

Hassell and Hassell, *History of the Church of God*, 834). For short descriptions of customs surrounding horse trade, shoots, fights, and muster days, see John Preston Arthur, *Western North Carolina: A History, 1730–1913*, ch. 11, "Manners and Customs" (Raleigh: Edwards and Broughton Print Company, 1914).

reproved a man in 1796 for going to horse races, and the following year it again cited the same man for charges related to a course race. In 1805–1806 a man was continued "with sharp reproof" after letting his horse run in a race. As with intoxication and violence, this type of recreation was acceptable for society's "ladies and gentlemen," and Anglican gentry encountered little opposition from their churches, but such behavior was out of order for Baptist church members, who were in subjection to a different standard.

Another charge that was usually brought against male members was that of Sabbath breaking. Article 7 of the Mechanicsville Church Covenant condemned making the Lord's day "a day of preparing for the business of the week, or of bestowing and receiving idle visits, spending the time allotted of the Lord for special worship in carnal feasting and some, we learn, have even prostituted the day to hunting, shooting, fishing & c." Turkey Creek even went so far in 1809 as to send the association a query whether it was permissible to marry on the Sabbath. The Cashaway and Mechanicsville Covenants condemned breaking the Sabbath, for example, with unnecessary river travel. Welsh Neck, in addition, ordered in October 1759 that "if any member travels up or down the river on a Sabbath-day without an absolute necessity (of which the Church shall be Judge) such member shall be censured." In the spring of 1807, several Skewarkey men asked forgiveness for "fishing on the Lord's Day."

Cases involving drunkenness, vulgarity, violence, and sporting all illustrate the insistence of churches that men, as well as women, were to be in subjection to God and to their church. Much of society winked at male drunkenness. Although churches allowed members to use intoxicating beverages in moderation, men were not at liberty to become drunk. Likewise, society permitted some violence, especially among males, as a matter of honor. But churches disciplined men for all types of violence; it was dishonorable regardless of class, reason, or target. And although gentlemen (and sometimes ladies as well) could participate in dancing, racing, and gambling, churches permitted neither for the men and women of their membership. These types of discipline cases overwhelmingly dealt with male offenders. This shows that, instead of enforcing a double standard that discriminated against women, churches strove to check society's permissiveness of male behavior.

4

FELLOWLABOURERS

No doubt most eighteenth-century household finances were in the hands of men. But as some historians have demonstrated, it is inaccurate to force men and women of the time into rigid "separate spheres" of public and private affairs. Church records suggest that, although men dominated money matters, sometimes women also claimed some financial opportunity and responsibility. And when such responsibility was betrayed, men and women alike were punished for their unfaithful stewardship. Churches expected members to support the ministry and their families. They were not to gamble with their money but to be good stewards. They were expected to be industrious six days of the week, but Sunday was to be set aside for rest and worship. Their business practices had to be honest, and even the relationship between a master and his human property (chattel slavery) was under the church's supervision. In matters of money and property, as in other matters, all church members were to be in subjection.

In *The Gentleman's Daughter*, Amanda Vickery found in journals of well-to-do ladies of eighteenth-century England evidence that public and private spheres overlapped in their lives. Lorri Glover found similar evidence in her study of South Carolina. But to an even greater extent, less prosperous American women found themselves involved in the world of work and money. For indentured servants and farmers' wives, this employment was both normal and necessary.[1] Churches and families could not often afford to place women on a pedestal of luxury. Akin to the "virtuous woman" King Solomon described in Proverbs 31, the Southern woman of virtue was industrious. In addition to keeping her home in order, she could also be found participating in the market economy as a means of providing for her family. Churches usually recognized this reality, at least during this time period. The only discipline case concerning a working woman was the one in which Welsh Neck suspended a woman for selling liquor at a horse race. It is likely that the circumstances of her business, not the fact that she was engaging in business, that was objectionable. For men and women alike, financial affairs were regulated, not condemned, by churches.

In the Bible, church members are taught that they are responsible for giving a tithe, or ten percent, of their worldly goods for the upkeep of the church. This responsibility was mandatory in eighteenth-century Southern churches, but how it was carried out varied depending on individual circumstances. Tithes were assessed, collected, spent, and recorded in various ways, but the basic principle of tithing was simple: each member owed an equal ten percent, from the widow's mite to the planter's pound. Of course, as heads of households, the responsibility for paying a family's tithe usually fell on husbands

---

[1] See Amanda Vickery, *The Gentleman's Daughter: Women's Lives in Georgian England* (New Haven: Yale University Press, 1998); Lorri Glover, *All Our Relations: Blood Ties and Emotional Bonds among the Early South Carolina Gentry* (Baltimore: Johns Hopkins University Press, 2000); Lois Carr and Lorena Walsh, "The Planter's Wife: The Experience of White Women in Seventeenth-Century Maryland," *William and Mary Quarterly*, 3d ser., 34 (1977); and Julia Cherry Spruill, *Women's Life and Work in the Southern Colonies* (Chapel Hill: University of North Carolina Press, 1938) ch. 12–14.

and fathers, but the church records make it clear that women were also expected to do their share.

Most of the church record books are sketchy in their general descriptions of financial dealings, but entries occasionally discuss both the principle of financial support and the practical matter of collection. Eaton's agreed in July 1773 that the "church should bear its own expenses and that on our monthly meeting before our communion season it is agreed that contribution should be made among the brethren for to defray the charges." Lick Fork agreed in 1811 that "the Preachers had a claim against the layety for a support not as a deed of charity or duty only but as a debt due from them to their Preachers." In Article 6 of the Mechanicsville Covenant, members promised to support their pastor, "contributing according as the Lord may have blessed us, freely to his support, recollecting that the Lord loveth a cheerful giver."

Although all churches agreed on the principle of tithing, methods of collecting tithes varied among congregations. Sometimes members bore the responsibility for assessing their own tithes, and sometimes churches appointed deacons or tithing committees to oversee the business.[2] Tithes were sometimes paid in cash, but they were also paid in produce, labor, or other goods. Yadkin members tithed in both currency and produce in 1791. Turkey Creek expected its members to contribute 25 cents each in 1805. Brier Creek in September 1818 "thought proper to put their produce into the hands of the deacon to supply the calls of the church." In July 1811 Tyger ordered members to

---

[2] Sandy Run established a tithing committee in Article 9 of its covenant. In July 1778, Eaton's put deacons in charge of raising a "bounty" for the support of its new pastor William Cook. Poplar Spring agreed in April 1794 to contribute quarterly to the church fund, and the following year the church established a committee to pay the pastor's salary.

"give produce into the hands of the deacons to sell and raise money for the support of the church" twice a year, in December and July. Bear Creek members settled the church's charges in 1792 with corn and wheat.

In 1800 the First Woodruff minutes included an assessment of each member's expected contribution. Nine of the twenty-one members listed were women. None of them was assessed as much as a pound, but then only three of the men were assessed at that amount. In all the church collected just over ten pounds for the year. Each member, male or female, was expected to tithe on whatever property they possessed, however little that amount might be. In December 1802, Poplar Spring answered a query affirming that it was right for every member to contribute according to ability. "Every member" clearly included females. The church's minutes for 1796 include a contributions chart and mention of "females that find it their bounden duty to contribute." In October of 1798, brethren who "put in mites for the fund" were listed by name.[3] Female contributors were rarely listed by name, but women of considerable means are occasionally noted in some record books. In April 1768, for example, Mrs. Daniel Devonalds "signed a Deed to Gift of Two Acres of Land whereon the [Welsh Neck meeting house was] situated." And in autumn 1747, Susannah Baker's contribution received recognition in the record book. In 1801, Sister Andrews joined three male members of Poplar Spring in contributing equally to the association fund.

Skewarkey's record book provides an unusually detailed account of the church's financial dealings.[4] A primary concern was supporting the pastor. In the autumn of 1787, a motion was made for Pastor Martin Ross's support, and a man was

[3] See Poplar Spring's financial records 1817–1820.

[4] Skewarkey was careful to maintain records. See special bookkeeping instructions given in 1792, 98, 07.

appointed to collect a subscription for the minister. In March 1788, a motion was made that the women of the church get the pastor a new suit of clothes. In June 1789, the church ordered that the pastor "have pork provided for his family's use." It also determined in December to give the pastor "a certain sum annually and that he have cloth bought immediately by some one of the deacons" for new clothing. The following month, the cloth was purchased for a new "great coat," and members were expected to pay their subscriptions. In July 1791, the deacons looked into purchasing a horse for their pastor to ride to an association meeting in Virginia. In July 1792, another reference is made to the yearly subscription for the pastor, and in December members were to pay in corn or pork, as the "deacons think sufficient." In 1793, the deacons proportioned members to pay a "note of hand" given by the pastor and another man in behalf of the church. Upon payment of their part, members were to have their credit recorded. One man was exempted from his note proportional "by reason of affliction" in July. In July 1795, the church ordered deacons to exhibit property assessments yearly. In August, the church called on members to contribute towards the pastor's support in corn and pork. The church determined that "each male member with such widows as are in circumstances sufficient be proportioned by committee." And in September, the church answered a query by affirming that no member was too poor to contribute. In 1798, the new pastor Luke Ward was expected to keep property assessments. In February 1803, the church ordered that it was the duty of male members to support the pastor, in March "each member" was to "put in quarterly" for the pastor's support, and in April "every person" was to "feel free" to contribute. Deacons, as was customary, reported their assessments in June. In February 1805, deacons were asked to "exhibit auts" quarterly. In November and December 1808, delegates from neighboring churches met to discuss pastoral support and determine proper amounts.

Of course, pastoral support was only one financial obligation for a church to consider. Certain spiritual responsibilities were also tied to financial considerations. Some church records make mention of purchasing wine for use as an element in the observance of the Lord's Supper.[5] Eaton's also provided a table in 1773, and Poplar Spring bought "two earthen cups" in 1799. Churches sometimes also considered giving financial support to itinerant missionaries and association funds.[6]

Another concern was securing and maintaining a meetinghouse, although it was not unusual for a church to meet in a member's home. Reedy River prepared a subscription to raise money for a new meetinghouse in 1818, and Jersey discussed doing so in 1796. In 1803 William Britton bequeathed a five acre land deed "for the sole use of the Baptist society Meeting House" at Sandy Run. In 1792, Poplar Spring appointed commissioners to "let a Baptist meeting house near Dunns Ford," and ten years later appointed a committee to pay a man for building a house. In June 1789, Skewarkey raised money to pay for "proving and registering the land deed." Once secured, a meetinghouse still needed to be furnished and maintained. In June 1804, Eaton's gave a brother detailed instructions for taking care of the new meeting house: "Bro. Thos. Crankfield was chosen to take care of the meeting house, to keep things decent and in order, also to take charge of all property left by the congregation through accident or forgetfulness so that the owner may have it again."

---

[5] Such is the case for Eaton's Baptist Church, Mocksville, NC (1776, 1778) and Skewarkey Baptist Church, Martin Co. NC (1787, 1788, 1812, 1814).

[6] See Poplar Spring Baptist Church, Zebulon NC (1789, 1799, 1801, 1804) and Skewarkey Baptist Church, Martin Co. NC (1788–1789, 1790, 1793–1794).

In July of 1788, Skewarkey appointed a committee for settling the church "auts" and assessing members, informing them of their "proportionals" for repairing the meetinghouse. It gave a contract to the lowest bidder to repair the house and add a shed the following year. In August 1789, each member was ordered to pay a "proportional" for repair work, and a committee was put in charge of assessments. In September one man was granted an exemption because his house had burned, and another due to his poverty. But another man was called to appear before a meeting of the church for not paying his part. And owing a debt to a Mr. Jenkins, the church assessed members in December to raise his payment.

Often male members were called upon to pay a tithe in labor by doing maintenance work themselves. Skewarkey's male members were regularly assigned to work on the building in July. Examples of these gender-specific tasks included "shrubbing" bushes, repairing seats, tarring the meetinghouse, repairing shingles, securing doors and windows, and digging wells. In 1790, Skewarkey contracted men to repair seats in the meetinghouse. The workmen did an "unfavorable" job, and when they refused to repair the seats properly at the church's request, the church decided to have the male members repair the seats themselves, "rather than enter into a disagreeable lawsuit." In February 1806, the church determined to employ others to build a pulpit and shingle the meetinghouse shed, but in March the church decided instead that the male members should do the work themselves. In 1810, a brother repaired the church well. He refused to accept payment, but the church paid his black assistant. Three years later, the church voted to have a new well dug on its own land, and male members were asked to pay the expense.[7]

Just as members were expected to provide for the material needs of the church, heads of families were expected to provide for their own to the best of their ability. In August 1806, two Tyger men made an allegation against a brother "for not taking a prudent care for his family." After laboring with the man, the church admonished him to mend his ways in the future. Again in March 1811, Tyger charged a brother with not providing sufficient support for his family. The man failed to give the church satisfaction, instead sending "harsh messages," and was excommunicated. In autumn 1793, Eaton's considered the matter that the mother of one of its males was dependent upon public relief, or in the church's language, "on the county." The church proposed that the man take his mother "off the county" by the end of the year. If, however, this "should make too much uneasiness at home," the church would provide for her in his place. The son initially rejected the proposal, but when the church suggested asking sister churches for advice in the matter, he reconsidered. Since the son was able to support his mother, the church considered it a matter of its own honor that he would fulfill his responsibilities. Had he not been able, the church would have stepped in to avoid the shame of having "the county" do the church's job.

A man's financial responsibility for his family was part of the moral economy's expectation that he be in subjection to his church's code of honor. Of course, in some situations fathers and sons were unable to support their families. As seen in Eaton's offer to family described above, churches frowned upon having members dependent upon public support, considering it

---

[7] See Skewarkey Baptist Church, Martin Co. NC, minutes for 1790, 1792–1795, 1802, 1806–1807, and 1810 for examples of July duties.

shameful for a church to fail to take care of its own. In 1792 Bush River "Agreed to contribute to the necessities of the poor brethren and requested the deacons of the church to attend to this business." The Bible instructs churches to provide for "widows that are widows indeed (1 Tim 5:3-4, 8, 16)."[8] If, however, a widow had children who could support her, the responsibility was theirs. A widow "indeed" was one who was truly desolate and had no family but her church to support her. Sons and daughters were to take care of their widowed mothers so that the church would be free to support those who had no family.

Public welfare of eighteenth-century America had roots in centuries of English precedent. Beginning in the sixteenth century, King Henry VIII responded to plague, enclosure, and the disestablishment of the Roman Catholic Church by transferring the responsibility of caring for the poor to the parish (the smallest unit of local government). A mandatory "poor rate" tax soon replaced the old voluntary church tithe, and leaders began to consider requiring the able-bodied poor to register with their parishes and work for their assistance. The new system took definite shape under the Elizabethan Poor Law at the beginning of the seventeenth century. By the late eighteenth century, England followed the philosophies of Adam Smith and Malthus

[8] "Honour widows that are widows indeed. But if any widow have children or nephews, let them learn first to shew piety at home, and to requite their parents: for that is good and acceptable before God.... But if any provide not for his own, and specially for those of his own house, he hath denied the faith, and is worse than an infidel.... If any man or woman that believeth have widows, let them relieve them, and let not the church be charged; that it may relieve them that are widows indeed" (1 Tim 5:3-4, 8, 16 KJV).

by viewing poor laws as an unhealthy encouragement of sloth, vice, and overpopulation.[9]

As in England, parish or county governments administered early American poor laws. In heavily populated areas such as Boston and Philadelphia, struggling newcomers could be "warned out," or prevented from settling and becoming a burden to the taxpayers. The poor and their children were subject to being auctioned off or forced into an apprenticeship or a workhouse. In Virginia illegitimate children of poor relief recipients could be "bound out" (i.e., indentured) according to a 1769 law. As illustrated in the vestry minutes of St. David's Parish in the Cheraw District of South Carolina, much "church business" revolved around collecting taxes, "binding out," and overseeing the poor.[10] According to Lucy Komisar, laws were friendlier in the South, where places of "indoor relief" (i.e., poor houses) were more common.[11] Nevertheless, churches felt responsibility for taking care of their own.

In 1812 Skewarkey considered a query whether "when a member is in distress and not capable of procuring natural subsistence…is it the duty of the church to relieve them, or shall they become a parishoner[?]" The query was laid over, and after "long discourse" was withdrawn the following month without a conclusion. It is unclear what circumstances were behind the 1812 debate, but the history of Skewarkey and other churches indicates a very clear position on the matter: churches should provide if families could not. In the 1780s Skewarkey continually called on its members to support the "lame Brother Blount." Members assisted him by providing firewood, money,

---

[9] Lucy Komisar, *Down and Out in the USA: A History of Social Welfare* (New York: Franklin Watts, 1973) ch. 1.

[10] *St. David's Parish Vestry Minutes 1768–85*, South Carolina Department of Archives and History, Columbia SC.

[11] Komisar, *Down and Out in the USA*, ch. 2.

provisions, and labor in the winter of 1786–1787. The brother was asked to keep account of services rendered. The following winter, church members were again called upon to contribute towards the brother's upkeep, and he was to exhibit his accounts at the end of the following year. In August 1788, the church resolved to provide him with "four barrels of corn, some pork, five days work in winter to get fire wood might suffice." As usual, the brother continued to exhibit his "auts" at the end of each year in proof that he had been provided for.

In September 1817, Abraham Belew of Reedy River "was presented to the Church as to know whether he was one of the poor of the Church or not, the Deacons was then appointed to go and search in to their standing and report to the Church whether this old Brother and wife comes under the appelation of the poor of the church yea or nay."[12] The deacons likely took into consideration information such as the plat of 372 acres he appears to have obtained on a branch of the South Pacolet River.[13] Tyger considered three such cases in 1806–1808. In June 1806, the church considered whether the contentious sister Hannah Belew came under the appellation "poor of the church" and looked into her circumstances. In August, allegation was made against John Belew "for not taking a prudent care for his family." In December, Hannah again "made application for support," and a brother of the church was appointed to "look into her affairs she given her self up to the tuition of the church." The next month the brother appointed made charge against her on behalf of church, at which she threw an angry fit and was censured. In June 1808, the same man laid in another allegation

---

[12] The result of this inquiry does not appear to have been recorded, but shortly thereafter a woman of the same last name was excommunicated for being found pregnant while single.

[13] South Carolina Department of Archives and History, Columbia SC.

against her, but when some brethren looked into her circumstances, the church "concluded she is not out of the poor of the church as yet."

Discipline cases concerning financial matters certainly were not limited to men failing to support their families. As seen in chapter 3, offenses involving money, such as gambling and Sabbath breaking, were matters of strict discipline. Just as horse races, shooting matches also found disfavor among churches due to the presence of gambling. And, once again, men were far more likely than women to be accused of participating in shooting matches. A Clear Springs query in October 1804 asking, "May members of our church send their property to a shooting match to be shot for[?]" was answered, "they may not." In September 1813, the church suspended a man "for putting in money at a shooting match and holding himself justifiable." Skewarkey excommunicated a man in March 1804 for "putting a turkey to be shot for." No form of gambling was acceptable. In July 1808, the church dealt with a man "for gambling or giting someon to gamble for him." The next month, at the recommendation of a committee, the church voted to excommunicate him for gambling. In 1796–1797, Eaton's considered a motion "respecting the lawfulness of Christians concerning in any ways with private lottery" and concluded it "to be a species of gambling, therefore inexpedient for Christians."

Any business conducted on the Sabbath (recognized by most Christians as Sunday) was considered disorderly by civil authority, as well as by church rules. In 1741, for example, a North Carolina statute proclaimed,

> Whereas in well-regulated governments effectual care is always taken that the day set aside for public worship be observed and kept holy; and, to suppress vice and immorality, Wherefore...be it enacted...that all and every person and persons whatsoever shall, on the Lord's Day, commonly called Sunday, carefully apply themselves to the duties of religion and piety; and that no tradesman, artisan, planter, laborer, or

> other person whatsoever, shall upon the land or water do or exercise any labor, business, or work of their ordinary calling, (works of charity and necessity only excepted) nor employ themselves either in hunting, fishing, or fowling, nor use any game, sport, or play, on the Lord's Day aforesaid, or any part thereof, upon pain that every Person so offending, being of the age of fourteen years and upwards, shall forfeit and pay the sum of ten shilling."[14]

Similar laws against Sabbath breaking were in effect throughout the colonies with minor variations. In collaboration with civil authorities, churches also enforced Sunday restrictions in the name of their God-given authority.

Clear Springs suspended one man between May and September 1805 for "misconduct such as sabbath breaking and other disorder," and excommunicated another man in August 1818 "for sabbath breaking and many other atrocious crimes." How, specifically, could a member "break the Sabbath"? One way was simply to deny its sanctity. A man who joined Eaton's in May 1802 caused difficulty "respecting the observation of the Lord's day" the next year, and in January 1804 "droped out of union for his obstinate refusing to comply with the rules and admonishions of the church and strenuously contending against the observance of the Lord's day, to the dishonor of the cause of God and grief of his brethren." Brushy Creek dealt with a man in 1799 for "grinding on the sabbath" and his heretical denial that there was a Sabbath. More often, members were charged with conducting inappropriate business on the Lord's day without denying that it should be honored. Skewarkey dealt with a man in February 1811 for "telling a falsity and respecting going to town after brandy on the Lord's day." Bush River excluded a man in 1806 for drunkenness and "selling spiritous liquors on the Sabbath day." Reedy River forgave a man in February 1816

[14] Statutes of NC, 1741 North Carolina State Archives, Raleigh NC.

upon his giving satisfaction "for trading on the sabbath." Bush River condemned members for breaking the Sabbath in various ways: planting tobacco, killing a beef, traveling to market, simply "working," etcetera. Traveling itself, apart from any connection with commerce, was frowned upon. In 1805 the church issued a statement agreeing that it was "inconsistent with the purity of the gospel for church members to set on a journey on Saturday or on the Sabbath with their waggons except in cases of real necessity."

Other discipline cases involved dishonest business practices that would have been condemned any day of the week. Tyger's Rules of Church Discipline declared that disputes between members "touching temporal concerns" should be brought before and decided by the church, since Scripture forbade members to sue each other in court.[15] Members also were expected to consult with the church before suing anyone. For example, Yadkin suspended a man in 1793 for "runing his neighbors unnessecerily in to the law." Lick Fork was "grieved" in 1805 when one brother obtained a search warrant against another.

One major category of business cases involved real estate. In September 1796, Brier Creek excommunicated a man for getting angry, behaving out of character, and "joining in with land speculators." Poplar Spring excommunicated a man in May 1804 for, among other things, "giving his son a tract of land and taking it away." In February 1792, Skewarkey arbitrated a land dispute between Edward Byrd and Jess Pierce. In autumn 1803, one man accused another of "using violence in preventing him from his labour," a puzzling charge that also turned out to be a land dispute. The men chose men of the church to settle the controversy. In December 1804 the church asked three men in a land dispute to show their deeds to a church committee. In

[15] 1 Cor 6:1-11.

March 1805, a committee was sent to "try to effect reconciliation" between the three men and one of their wives, "having expressed themselves dissatisfied at the line made between their lands by the committee," which had apparently ruled in favor of William Biggs. The committee was unable to effect reconciliation, and two of the men were excommunicated for "not abiding by their agreement made before conference," and the wife of one was excommunicated "for refractory language in conference against" the man in whose favor the church ruled. Apparently church members even answered to their church for their dealings with renters and squatters; in 1806 a Lick Fork man "reported concerning pushing [another man] out of his house." The church seems to have approved, for "it was looked over."

Another matter was defrauding creditors. In November 1813, Reedy River considered a query whether it was agreeable for a professor of Christianity "to take his sons property and keep it so that his sons creditors cannot come at there own rite." The church answered in the negative and thought proper to inquire into the circumstances. In November 1815, a man had to give the church satisfaction that, contrary to a charge against him, "he had not put his property out of his hands in order to defraud his creditors."

Churches also arbitrated rent disputes. In December 1812, a Tyger man charged John Belew and his wife Polly "for some contempt they had offered to some of their brethren and neighbors about an arbitration between themselves and Hannah Belew." The following month, Hannah charged John with "not complying with the reward given her by arbitration in consequence of rent and some other small dealings."[16] She later agreed to be patient with him, and he was to "comply with their

[16] See earlier mention of Belew family in ch. 2.

former contracts." At the same time, a brother raised the question what the church should do with members "who neglect to pay their just debts."

Like many other churches, Skewarkey Baptist Church often found it necessary to discipline members for failing to pay their debts. In June 1788, two Skewarkey brethren were cited to explain why they had failed to pay a subscription to another brother. In June 1790, William Biggs inquired into "pursuing legal steps of the law to recover money owed him," as executor of an estate, by members of the church. The church said it was "not agreeable to God's word until he had hearing before the church." The church experienced such "great difficulties" that for a time it considered itself "not in order to commune." The following January, the man was excommunicated, and all church members indebted to him were ordered to pay quickly. In July 1791, the minutes state that he was excommunicated for "going to law with brother over money." In July 1805, two men were cited for nonpayment of money to two other men, and the matters were settled peacefully by September. Between February and May 1806, the church worked to make peace between two brethren, one owing the other money. And between October and November, a debt was settled between two other men. In December, Kedar Biggs asked the church "how he should proceed with members indebted to him as executor to a deceased person's estate that neglected payment," and the church ordered "that he be at liberty to pursue the regular steps of the law but in a christian like manner."

Churches were not to 'keep company' with offenses such as covetousness and extortion (1 Corinthians 5). In November 1803, Eaton's considered the query, "what is extortion" The church answered, "any advantage of our necessity."

The most common type of extortion case involved the price of grain. Turkey Creek, for example, set a maximum price in 1786 for which members could sell corn and wheat. Corn could not sell for more than two shillings per bushel. A Shoal Creek man denied the charge of selling corn for one dollar per bushel in 1776. At the same time the church considered an accusation of selling wheat at an extortionate price, but the church at Shoal Creek concluded that it was not authorized to set a certain price. In July 1807, a Tyger man was charged with "selling corn at one dollar per bushel." A committee of brethren appointed to decide the matter convinced the church to excommunicate him the following month. In July 1804, a member of Clear Springs "moved that the church consider members selling corn at an extortionate price," and the following month the church answered, "we can set no certain price upon corn. But advise our members to be careful in that point." South Fork of Roaring River reproved a man in 1786 for selling corn at £20 per barrel. He agreed to pay back £5 and never repeat the offense. In 1796, a woman accused a man of the church of extortion, but she herself was cited for "not dealing with him agreable to the gospel" in neglecting to discuss the business with him in private before bringing it before the church.

The high price of grain was not the only form of extortion. Horse trading was also a common target for charges of extortion. The sale of alcohol was approved only under certain circumstances. In May 1802, Reedy River answered a query "whether a man selling liquor without license shall be held in fellowship" in the negative. Churches also disapproved of members providing liquor to the public "by the small." Bush River, for example, considered the following query in 1806: "is it a matter worthy of censure for brethren to carry or send spirituous liquors to publick places to sell by the small[?] Answer we think it is a practice beneath the dignity of a disciple of Jesus and that it is not sanctioned by the gospel."

No discussion of economic matters in the South during this time would be complete without a discussion of slavery. According to David Benedict, the Baptist position on the subject of slavery was ambiguous: "The Baptists are by no means uniform in their opinions of slavery. Many let it alone altogether; some remonstrate against it in gentle terms; others oppose it vehemently; while far the greater part of them hold slaves, and justify themselves the best way they can."[17] That slavery was present in many of these congregations is evident in the church records. Naturally, it was more widespread in some areas than others. The Sandy Run membership list separated members' names not only by gender but also by color, as well as slave and free blacks, and in 1799 the record book mentions separate "negro services." Occasionally male slaves were licensed to preach. Evidence of slavery in some churches is found in references to the baptism of a "servant" or "negro."[18] Ashley River even bought four black slaves for its pastor in August 1768 and resold them the following year, after removing the pastor from office. Jersey also purchased a slave for its pastor in August 1795.

Slaves were sometimes defendants in church discipline cases. In August 1812, Tyger excommunicated a female slave "for seling her masters property to travellers in the absence of her master and mistress contrary to their orders and disposing of the money to her own use, and as [she] was sent to tennessee before they had a opportunity to deal with her they certify the whole matter to a church there to deal with her…" In June 1821, a Brier Creek man informed the church that "he had been very much difficultied conserning of his negro [who] in the first place disobeyed his orders and then being guilty of getting very angry with another of my negros and pased blows between them, it was put to the church to know whether they could approbate

---

[17] David Benedict, *A General History of the Baptist Denomination in America*, vol. 2 (Boston: Lincoln & Edmands, 1813) 207.

[18] See Skewarkey 1802 and Welsh Neck 1770s for revival-period examples.

such conduct as that." The church thought not, and when cited, the slave "said the charge was just and he had been very much distressed about it and had a hope that the Lord had forgive him for it," and was restored. In January 1793, a man of Poplar Springs cited his male slave to answer a charge of "stealing brandy and drinking same." The slave was restored in March. In January 1804, Skewarkey excommunicated a black man for "procuring a forged pass and running away."

The institution of slavery came with expectations for white men as well. They were not to harbor runaway slaves, use excessive physical force, or compel a slave to work on Sundays. Masters were sometimes charged in cases involving slavery. In January 1815, Clear Springs considered in a query whether a master may "correct a slave by stripes [whipping] when both are members of the same church," answering "we think a man may correct his slave if necessity calls for it but at next meeting lay the matter before the church in order that such disobedient slaves may be delt with the church." In July 1807, a Brier Creek woman "laid in a grievance" against a man "concerning a report that he had put out about her abusing her slaves." The man acknowledged that "he had wronged the sister by reporting this from groundless authority." In May 1793, a Skewarkey man was charged with "making a boy that is bound to him cut and hawl fire wood on the sabbath," but the man was retained as a member. A Skewarkey man was charged with "hiring negroe slaves to work for him on the Lord's Day" in summer 1804. The man was retained after the church heard testimony and discussed the charges. In July 1805, a man was excommunicated "for dishonesty with respect to his conduct in trade with a certain man of colour," compounded with the "fist of wickedness" and false testimony.

These cases illustrate the expectation that all church members—male or female, black or white—show responsibility for whatever earthly goods they possessed. Men and women worked side by side, although their tasks were not identical. Farming families worked together to raise crops and livestock, a portion of which would go towards their church tithe for the minister's support. If the meetinghouse or grounds needed maintenance work, the men would bring their tools. If the pastor needed a new suit, the women would make it. Church members were to be good stewards, not wasting their money foolishly on gambling. They were not to let covetousness cause them to break the Sabbath or take advantage of others through extortion. They were to honor their contracts, large or small. Slaves were required to respect a master's property rights, but masters too were regulated in their dealings with slaves. Unlike civil courts, church business meetings allowed slaves to testify, occasionally even against white members. Property and power were clearly unequal, yet even masters were held accountable and placed in subjection to the rules of the churches.

Although the slave population was comparable between Low Country North and South Carolina, and slavery's presence can be seen in most churches, the institution appears to have had an especially significant impact on the economy (financial and moral) of Welsh Neck. George Johnson's community study followed the history of the Welsh Neck community in the Cheraw/Darlington County area of South Carolina from its "frontier" settlement by Welsh migrants beginning in the 1730s and tracing its growth and integration into the South Carolina Low Country through the eighteenth century. In the 1730s, South Carolina's governor Robert Johnson implemented a plan to establish eleven townships along what was then the "frontier" of European settlement in the royal colony. The system of townships was intended to be a buffer to protect Low Country whites from Indian raids and slave uprisings. To encourage settlement of the townships, South Carolina offered incentives that attracted people from the Pennsylvania region and elsewhere.

Among the first to settle the area that would become Darlington County were a group of Welsh Baptists from Delaware. They successfully petitioned for a land grant in 1736, which included eight miles of land on each side of the Pee Dee River extending northward from Queensboro. They likely traveled by boat to Charles Town and then on to Georgetown, where each family head was welcomed with a supply of corn, salt, pork, livestock, and tools, compliments of the township fund. In addition, each settler over the age of twelve was entitled to fifty acres of land, and new families could take advantage of a ten-year tax deferment. They were also eligible for subsidies to promote mills. Welsh Baptists such as John Kolb of Cashaway, who built a corn mill, became actively involved in the regional flour trade.

Prior to 1760, Welsh settlers dominated the region; their culture, language, and religion saw little competition from other groups. As late as 1759, sixty of sixty-five surnames on the membership list of Welsh Neck Baptist Church were Welsh. During the 1760s, an influx of English, German, and Scots-Irish began arriving from other parts of the South and along the Great Wagon Road from Pennsylvania. By 1779, less than a quarter of the church membership was Welsh. Even in the earliest days in their new home, however, the Welsh Baptists were not alone; some of the first settlers brought slaves with them to South Carolina. It can be deduced from the taxes paid on imported slaves on June 20, 1738, that six men together imported seventeen slaves. Johnson estimates that the population of the Welsh Neck community included 500 whites and 60 slaves in 1747. By the 1790 census, there were 7,418 whites and 3,229 slaves.[19] Despite the fact that slaves made up about a third of the

[19] George L. Johnson, *The Frontier in the Colonial South: South Carolina Backcountry, 1736–1800* (Westport CT: Greenwood Press, 1997) ch. 1, Table 1.2, 21, 81.

population, most white inhabitants of the Welsh Neck community were not slaveholders. As late as 1790, 72 percent of the households reported in the federal census included no slaves. Seventeen percent of households owned between one and five slaves; approximately 5 percent owned between six and ten slaves, and approximately 2 percent owned between eleven and fifteen slaves. Of the 2 percent that held more than sixteen slaves, only eight of thirty-seven households owned more than forty-five slaves.[20]

That minority of slaveholders, however, managed to accumulate significant wealth, especially through the production of indigo and, to a greater extent after the Revolution, corn, tobacco, and eventually cotton. Estate inventories show that they lived comfortable lives rivaling that of the coastal elite.[21] Furthermore, the slaveholding elite enjoyed positions of considerable influence. During the first decades of settlement, Welsh Neck members did not tend to be extremely wealthy. In the 1750s, for example, Pastor Philip James raised livestock on a 350-acre estate and owned one female slave. John Evans employed one slave family in raising corn and wheat on his 300-acre estate valued at £1,344. In the 1760s, David Harry's estate was valued at only £287 with no slaves, and in the 1770s Pastor Nicholas Bedgegood owned 350 acres and fifteen slaves. As early as the 1760s, some members of the Welsh Neck congregation amassed considerable fortunes through the use of slave labor. Robert Williams (one of the first pastors) accumulated fifty slaves and an estate of more than 3,000 acres valued at over £23,000. In the 1770s, his son David raised indigo on a 3,000-acre estate with the labor of seventy-six slaves (twenty families). Robert's son-in-law Arthur Hart, who was a justice of the peace and member of Black Creek

[20] Johnson, *The Frontier in the Colonial South*, 81; 1790 Census, North Carolina State Archives, Raleigh NC.

[21] Johnson, *The Frontier in the Colonial South*, ch. 2–3.

Baptist Church, raised indigo on a 750-acre estate valued over £20,000 with the help of twenty-eight slaves.[22] Evan Pugh, who was pastor of Welsh Neck and Cashaway in the 1760s, worked as a surveyor under George Washington as a boy in Virginia and later taught school. In South Carolina, he raised indigo on 700 acres, which yielded a hefty supplement to his annual pastoral salary of £700.[23]

In 1798 the church exchanged its humble meetinghouse on the eastern bank of the Pee Dee River for a new one on the Society Hill side, which was less susceptible to flooding. The new building was not extravagant, but it did include a porch, a separate section to seat slaves, pew rentals, and a high pulpit with a flight of steps and doors on each side. In 1843, it too was replaced by a large new building with a bell and tall steeple.[24] The church was moving up in the world.

George Johnson and Rachel Kline both emphasized Welsh Neck's integration into the economic and political life of coastal South Carolina. According to Kline, the slaveholding elite of coastal South Carolina and inland areas such as Welsh Neck forged early ties that did much to unify the state long before the cotton revolution. Simultaneous with this political and economic

[22] Ibid., 68–73.

[23] Ibid., 43; Eliza Cowan Ervin and Horace Fraser Rudisill, eds, *Darlingtoniana: A History of People, Places and Events in Darlington County, South Carolina* (Spartanburg: Reprint Company, 1997) 117; Horace Fraser Rudisill (transcriber), *The Diaries of Evan Pugh, 1762–1801* (Florence SC: St. David's Society, 1993).

[24] Ervin and Rudisill, *Darlingtoniana*, 112; See pictures of the 1843 building in Horace Fraser Rudisill, *Darlington County: A Pictorial History* (Norfolk: Donning Company, 1986) 27–28. Special thanks to the friendly folks I met at the Society Hill Library for their hospitality during my research trip in 2007. They even loaned me a flashlight when I visited the old church meeting site on the bank of the Pee Dee River at twilight, a highlight of my journey through the Carolinas.

integration, churches such as Welsh Neck also witnessed changes in their moral economy. Prosperity certainly did not necessarily equal apostasy, but as Southern churches developed closer ties with their secular world of political independence from white men and black slavery, the traditional system of subjection would become strained and its meaning contested. They faced new choices that, as will be seen in the areas of slavery and marriage, could undermine the shared values of mutual subjection that church discipline once upheld.

5

PROMISCUITY AND MARRIAGE

As seen in chapter 1, marriage symbolized the relationship between a church and its head, Jesus Christ. Just as churches owed him obedience in return for his love, husbands and wives were assigned mutual obligations. Their respective obligations, though different, required both to perform certain duties designed to honor the sanctity of matrimony. Once married, Christian couples were expected to glorify God with their family life. Article 10 of the Cashaway Baptist Church Covenant stated, "We mutually agree and promise that if God sho'd give us the charge of Children, that we will endeavour to bring them up in the Fear, Nurture and Admonition of the Lord, and in the same Principles and Faith which we now sign to."

A man of Tyger advised in 1804 that the eldership examine individual members and exhort them to the performance of family duty. In the Poplar Spring Covenant, members promised to watch over families and children under their care. A Flat River query of 1789 affirmed unanimously that "every master of a family ought to keep up the worship of God in his house." Skewarkey answered a 1787 query by recommending that family worship be practiced twice daily. In Article 5 of the Sandy Run Covenant, masters and mistresses of families agreed to keep up the worship of God in families by morning and evening prayer. The church would discipline members who omitted this duty.

The marriages of ministers were expected to serve as positive examples for the congregations under their care. The well known patriot, Oliver Hart of Charleston, wrote in his diary of his happy marriage with his second wife, Anne, after the death of his first wife, Sarah. Hart also memorialized fellow minister Francis Pelot as an exemplary family man, discussed the strains of the Revolutionary War on his own family, and mentioned his approval of his son's marriage to a girl of poverty.[1] Sandy Run recognized its late pastor Lemuel Burkitt in a written tribute to the pastor, husband, father, master, and republican. In a detailed biography of former clerk Kedar Biggs, Skewarkey recounted the story of his introduction to family worship and his and his wife's conversions.[2]

According to custom in the colonial South, it was preferable (although not necessary) that couples seek their parents' blessing before marriage.[3] Baptist churches expected their members to consult with them as well. Under the Anglican establishment in the colonial South, dissenting ministers were not authorized to perform marriage ceremonies. It appears from Tyger's records that Baptist churches expected their ministers to accept such

[1] Oliver Hart Diary, 1741–1780, Oliver Hart Papers, South Caroliniana Library, Columbia SC.

[2] Sandy Run 1807, and Skewarkey 1814.

[3] "The couple discovered one another in the usual ways, obtained the consent of their parents, had the banns published in the parish church, and were married by the local minister. They could forget their parents' consent—as far as the law was concerned—if the girl was over sixteen and the boy was twenty-one, but of course it was not good taste for children to proceed in these matters without their parents' advice" (Edmund Morgan, *Virginians at Home: Family Life in the Eighteenth Century* [Williamsburg: Colonial Williamsburg Foundation, 1952] 29–30). See Daniel Blake Smith, *Inside the Great House: Planter Family Life in Eighteenth-Century Chesapeake Society* (Ithaca: Cornell University Press, 1980) 132, on the absence of parental control in courtship.

limitations.[4] Although Baptist ministers could not perform marriages, Baptist churches did claim the right to regulate marriages. Baptist churches preferred that members marry within the faith, not being "unequally yoked" (2 Cor 6:14), but such was not always the case. There are a few discipline cases involving controversial marriages, but the church's disapproval is vague.[5] Baptist records do not resemble those of the Society of Friends or "Quakers," who spent much of their business meetings strictly examining candidates for marriage. For example, the Cane Creek Monthly Meeting in Union County, South Carolina, and the Bush River Monthly Meeting in Newberry County, South Carolina, had separate business meetings for the men and women. Their minute books reveal their diligence in inspecting marriage candidates before granting their approval of the union. The Bush River men's meeting shows male members examining prospective grooms when a couple declared their intent to wed, in addition to the usual disciplinary business of issuing "papers against" male members for offenses such as drinking, quarreling, and fighting. The Cane Creek women's meeting received women and children as members of the society and carried out discipline with "papers of condemnation" or "papers of testification against" offending members for offenses such as "bastardy" and "attending disorderly [unapproved] weddings." In addition, they were responsible for inspecting marriage candidates and sending the men's meeting correspondence regarding their approval or disapproval. When a woman went against the society's instructions and "married out of order," the women's meeting disowned her with the "approbation of the

---

[4] Showing respect for the laws of the land, the Tyger rules stated that ministers were not to go beyond the "limits of national government" in administering marriage. See also the September 1811 query on ministers acting as Justice of the Peace.

[5] See Tyger 1805, Clear Springs 1805.

men's meeting." Often, however, marriage proposals did meet with the society's approval. Minutes contain lengthy records detailing the Quaker marriage ceremonies. After properly publicizing their intent to marry, couples said their vows before a large company of friends and witnesses and promised to be loving and faithful until death. They then "set their hands" to confirm their vows.[6]

Baptist churches were usually not as diligent in screening prospective marriages, but they did actively regulate the behavior of couples and families after a marriage had taken place. Just as churches praised godly families, they also condemned those they saw as disorderly. Dancing, carnal music, card games, and general disorder had no place in a true Christian home. A Skewarkey man was charged in 1791 with "allowing his son that is under his tuition to go to Dancing School," the church inquiring "Whether profesors of Christianity were Justifiable in letting their children frequent Balls & other places of merriment." The church ruled that it was "by no means justifiable." The man later stated that he did not know about the dancing school, and since he had learned of it, he had done everything in his power to prevent it, which defense the church accepted. In 1811, the same church made inquiry about whether it should excuse "any Member who is a Master of a Family, that suffers Dancing in there house, & also allows themselves in the Practice of Playing Cards for diversion." The query was

[6] Cane Creek Monthly Meeting, Society of Friends, Women's Minutes, Union County SC, 1789–90 (South Carolina Department of Archives and History, Columbia SC); Bush River Monthly Meeting, Society of Friends, Men's Minutes, Newberry County SC, 1772 (South Carolina Department of Archives and History, Columbia SC). For more on Quaker family life, see Barry Levy, *Quakers and the American Family: British Settlement in the Delaware Valley* (New York: Oxford University Press, 1988).

answered in the negative, and a man was then charged with allowing the aforesaid activities in his home. In 1816, Brier Creek cited a man to answer for keeping a disorderly house, but he denied the charge and gave satisfaction.[7]

More commonly, the disorder that disturbed churches involved the relationship between couples, rather than how they ruled their households. Some cases are vague, such as marriages that stirred controversy without clear reasons. Other cases concern vague charges of "immorality."[8] Churches often reminded members in the Covenants that some matters should be kept private, and that the church was to be "a garden enclosed," not exposed shamelessly to the gossip of the world. The Poplar Spring Covenant, for example, stated that in addition to watching over and exhorting one another, members promised to "keep our own secrets, being taught by God's word that the church of Christ is a Garden enclosed, a spring shut up, a fountain sealed." But church records were usually specific about their grievances. This type of discipline case can be divided into three categories: fornication, marital disputes, and adultery.

Church and state alike punished both women and men for fornication in the seventeenth- and eighteenth-century American South. Writing of colonial laws against such offenses, Julia Cherry Spruill observed, "If multiplicity of restrictive laws could assure righteousness, all the women of easy virtue who came to the colonies would soon have been converted into models of continence." Such laws were often broken, especially by indentured servants who were not allowed to marry without the consent of their masters. Finding themselves outside the regulation of close family ties, indentured servants often formed "unconventional unions" which, if caught, were subject to legal

---

[7] See ch. 3 for the context of dancing and playing cards.

[8] For vague cases see Tyger Oct 05; Clear Springs Nov 05, also Skewarkey, Jersey, Eaton's, and Poplar Spring.

punishment. The Virginia House of Burgesses, for example, passed various acts imposing fines for fornication and adultery (adulterers were fined double), and declared that offenders who failed to pay the fine be whipped or imprisoned. In North Carolina, those charged with a first offense of fornication were fined fifty shillings or a maximum of twenty-one lashes; adulterers had to pay a fine of five pounds or face a similar whipping for the first offense.[9] In spite of such penalties, according to Bertram Wyatt-Brown, Southern society was very permissive of male fornication. Slave women and white women of low status were considered fair game.[10]

Colonial fornication laws also dealt specifically with cases involving illegitimate children. According to Spruill, lawmakers were "more intent upon saving their parishes from the upkeep of numerous bastards than concerned with the preservation of morality for its own sake." Throughout the Southern colonies, parents accused of bearing illegitimate children were required to give "security" that they would maintain the child at their own expense. Out of a total of twenty-seven of these "bastardy bonds" registered in Rowan County, North Carolina, between 1800 and 1810, in eight cases the mother is listed as primary bondsman, but in each case at least one male bondsman (two of them apparently the grandfathers) is also listed.[11] In South

[9] Julia Cherry Spruill cites several legal sources from Virginia and the Carolinas (*Women's Life and Work in the Southern Colonies* [Chapel Hill: University of North Carolina Press, 1938] 314–15).

[10] Bertram Wyatt-Brown, *Honor and Violence in the Old South* (New York: Oxford University Press, 1986) 96–97. This is an abridged version of *Southern Honor*.

[11] " When the pregnancy of a woman or birth of a child was brought to the attention of the court, a warrant was issued and the woman brought in to court. She was examined (questioned) under oath and asked to declare the name of the child's father. The reputed father

Carolina, the court took the mother's word concerning the child's father; an alleged father was presumed guilty until proven innocent. Accusations proven to be false, however, could be punished with whipping. If the father's identity was kept secret, the mother was held responsible for giving security and paying court fines; failure to pay would result in public whipping.[12]

In secular cases where a female defendant was an indentured servant, the master was also awarded payment for his temporary loss of labor. The servant would be assessed with a fine (paid to the master or to the government) or, more commonly, a lengthened term of service. In addition to their loss of labor, masters of servants who committed the crime of fornication sometimes had to pay the tobacco fine, which the servant would pay back with a lengthened indenture; if a master refused to pay a servant's fine, the servant would be whipped. When lawmakers recognized that such clauses invited abusive masters to rape their servants for a profit, they addressed the loophole with new laws stating that in such cases of rape by her master, the mother would be removed from the master and indentured to serve the parish instead.[13] Other laws punished the parents of mulatto offspring, whether or not they were married. Whites who married blacks could be banished. If the mothers were black, of course the children would be enslaved. If the mothers

---

was then served a warrant and required to post bond. If the woman refused to name the father, she, her father or some other interested party would post the bond. In some cases it was found that the mother and reputed father together posted the bond. If the woman refused to post bond or declare the father, she was often sent to jail" (Betty and Edwin Camin, *North Carolina Bastardy Bonds* [Mt. Airy NC: B. J. and E. A. Camin, 1990] introduction, 99).

[12] Spruill, *Women's Life and Work*, 315–23.

[13] Ibid., 317–21.

were white, on the other hand, they would be forced to pay a fine to the Anglican church wardens or be "disposed of" for five years. Lindman states that Virginia churches punished "interracial mixing," but none of the Carolina church discipline cases surveyed here make mention of intermarriage or mulatto offspring.[14]

According to Spruill, although colonial statutes called for equal punishments for men and women, in reality men were more likely to be able to pay fines if apprehended, while women most often faced corporal punishment. Colonial courts could exercise discretion in their leniency towards offenders, which sometimes worked in favor of male defendants. In some cases, fornicators and adulterers were simply admonished or ordered to do public penance before a church. In seventeenth-century Virginia, for example, a couple might be ordered to appear before a church in white sheets and repeat the confession,

> "I ___ and ___ do here acknowledge and confess in the presence of this whole congregation that I have grievously sinned and offended against the Divine Majesty of Almighty God and all Christian people in committing the foul and detestable sin of Adultery and am heartily sorry and truly penitent for the same and do unfeignedly beseech Almighty God of his infinite goodness to be merciful unto me and to forgive this my heinous offense and I do heartily desire this congregation and all good people likewise to forgive me and pray for me."[15]

Facing the prospects of public humiliation, fines, and corporal punishment, some women attempted to conceal their crime by destroying the evidence. Infanticide was much more

---

[14] Lindman, *A World of Baptists: Gender, Race, and Religious Community in Pennsylvania and Virginia, 1689–1825* (Minneapolis: University of Minnesota, 1994) 221.

[15] Spruill, *Women's Life and Work*, 339, 319–20.

common than abortion in America and throughout the world in the eighteenth and nineteenth centuries. According to Joseph Dellapenna, abortion was neither safe (for the mother), effective, nor morally acceptable. Methods of injury and intrusion were as dangerous to mothers as to the babies they carried, and ingestion techniques involved substances so ineffective that, if consumed in doses that would cause abortion, would also kill the mother. In addition, religious leaders and legal scholars agreed in their respect for unborn life.[16] Of the few women who chose to dispense with their offspring, most did so by means of infanticide. Southern colonies passed laws that prescribed the death penalty for mothers who concealed the birth and death of their children. Their attempt to conceal an infant's death was assumed to be evidence of infanticide.[17]

Englishmen such as Thomas Coram, William Hogarth, Jonathan Swift, and Daniel Defoe responded to their nation's crisis of illegitimacy and infanticide by advocating the establishment of a Foundling Hospital in London. Which approach was most effective: charity or chastisement?[18] In her literary study of England's "century of illegitimacy," Lisa Zunshine argues that in eighteenth-century England, the measures taken by religious and civil authorities against illegitimacy were counterproductive and even encouraged infanticide. Civil laws prescribed corporal punishment and imprisonment for mothers of illegitimate

---

[16] Joseph Dellapenna, *Dispelling the Myths of Abortion History* (Durham: Carolina Academic Press, 2006). A female criminal could be granted a reprieve of her sentence by "claiming her belly." If a jury of matrons confirmed that she was pregnant, her execution would be postponed until delivery to spare the life of the unborn child (Spruill, *Women's Life and Work*, 326).

[17] Spruill, *Women's Life and Work*, 324–25.

[18] Lisa Zunshine, *Bastards and Foundlings: Illegitimacy in Eighteenth-Century England* (Columbus: Ohio State University Press, 2005) ch. 2.

children, and incest and adultery were capital offenses. According to Zunshine, "the fear of corporal punishment and public ostracism would often prompt the unwed woman (particularly of the serving class) to conceal her pregnancy and try to get rid of the child as soon as it was born," even though another law stated that unwed mothers who concealed the birth and death of their children were guilty of infanticide. Anglican church courts also punished illegitimacy. Zunshine explains that church-enforced penance ranged from repenting in front of the congregation to being excommunicated and having baptism denied to the child. She suggests that in cases of church discipline, as with civil punishments, concern for her reputation could lead a woman to consider infanticide, risking the more serious consequences for the sin of murder.[19]

Besides fornication, adultery is also condemned as a serious sin throughout the Bible. In 1 Corinthians 5, churches are instructed to discipline members, male or female, who are guilty of the offense. But Bertram Wyatt-Brown suggests that Southern society frowned upon adulteresses while turning a blind eye to most white male adulterers. An adulteress was more commonly found among the lower or middle-class women, especially on the frontier, than among the closely supervised ladies of elite households. Although their society was less approving of them than of their male counterparts, their offense was "not a matter of criminal violation," at least after the Anglican Church was disestablished in the South following the American Revolution. Until the Revolutionary War, adultery fell under ecclesiastical jurisdiction by common law, but afterward Southern state governments refused to replace ecclesiastical laws with civil legislation penalizing sexual offenses.[20]

---

[19] Ibid., 42.

[20] Bertram Wyatt-Brown, *Honor and Violence in the Old South*, 99.

Several adultery cases found in church records may at first seem puzzling to modern readers because of churches' changing attitudes towards remarriage. Many eighteenth-century Baptists, along with many other Christians of the time, believed that divorce and remarriage constituted adultery; according to the Bible, only death can dissolve the marriage contract. This doctrine is crucial to understanding many discipline cases. Jesus commanded, "Whosoever putteth away his wife, and marrieth another, committeth adultery: and whosoever marrieth her that is put away from her husband committeth adultery" (Luke 16:18). He furthermore stated, "And if a woman shall put away her husband, and be married to another, she committeth adultery" (Mark 10:12).[21] The Apostle Paul also wrote of the lifelong indissolubility of marriage and the sin of adulterous remarriage.[22]

The doctrine of marital indissolubility long determined the laws of "Christian nations." The Church of England continued to hold to the doctrine in spite of the circumstances that led to its break with the Roman Catholic Church. Some Protestant groups in Europe began to allow divorce under circumstances such as adultery, abuse, desertion, and impotence in the sixteenth and

---

[21] See also Matt 5:32 and 19:3-9, where reference is made to an exception unique to the Jewish audience for "fornication" during the betrothal period.

[22] "For the woman which hath an husband is bound by the law to her husband so long a he liveth; but if the husband be dead, she is loosed from the law of her husband. So then if, while her husband liveth, she be married to another man, she shall be called an adulteress: but if her husband be dead, she is free from that law; so that she is no adulteress, though she be married to another man" (Rom 7:2-3); "And unto the married I command, yet not I, but the Lord, Let not the wife depart from her husband: But and if she depart, let her remain unmarried, or be reconciled to her husband: and let not the husband put away his wife" (1 Cor 7:10-11).

seventeenth centuries. The Puritans defied the instructions of the mother country by granting divorces in New England. In the Anglican Southern colonies, divorce was slow in taking root, but in the decades following the Revolution laws gradually accommodated divorce in the Southern states. Revolutionary rhetoric compared political tyranny to an abusive husband, arguing for the right of wronged wives and subjects to break their contracts of subjection. When values of independence seeped from the world of politics into the social order, they challenged those of subjection.[23]

When divorce did enter the region, as in England it could be obtained only by successfully petitioning the state legislature. Thomas Buckley's survey of legislative divorce petitions in Virginia shows that, of the hundreds of petitions by both men and women, only a third were granted. Buckley looks to the attitudes of church, state, and society to explain Virginia's hostility toward divorce, citing the anti-divorce writings of ministers such as Presbyterian George Bourne and Episcopalian Isaac Hite, and the measures churches of various denominations took against adultery. And although John Wesley made allowance for divorce and remarriage in cases of adultery, many American Methodists

[23] Roderick Phillips, *Putting Asunder: A History of Divorce in Western Society* (New York: Cambridge University Press, 1988); Jessica Flinchum, "Reluctant Revolutionaries: The Philadelphia Baptist Association and the American Revolution," *Pennsylvania History* 74/2 (Spring 2007): 177–78. E. P. Thompson writes of the English custom of "wife sales." Plebeians practiced this form of de facto divorce in spite of a legal institution that forbade it. It is possible that some Americans also used the wife sale in their attempt to justify remarriage ("The Moral Economy of the English Crowd in the Eighteenth Century," *Customs in Common: Studies in Traditional Popular Culture* [New York: The New Press, 1993] ch. 7).

rejected the practice regardless of the circumstances.[24] Just as Methodists, Presbyterians were not unanimous in their position regarding remarriage. Stoney Creek Independent Presbyterian Church in Prince William's Parish, South Carolina, for example, stated in its covenant and confession of the 1740s that marriage should be between one man and one woman, that no man ought to have more than one wife "at once." This "one-at-a-time" clause made allowance for remarriage after divorce.[25]

Following the same path as some church positions, civil law gradually gave way to demands for divorce, especially following the Revolution. State legislatures began granting divorce in North Carolina in 1794, in Georgia in 1798, in Tennessee in 1799, and in Virginia in 1803. North Carolina granted ten legislative divorces in the 1790s. The state law of 1814 allowed courts to grant divorce on grounds of adultery or impotence, and to grant women separations in cases of desertion, cruelty, or eviction. Alleged offenses had to have existed for six months prior to filing a divorce petition. Dissolution would not take effect for a year, and until 1818 the legislature had to confirm court decisions. Then the innocent party could remarry legally. By 1835 the courts handled all divorce cases in North Carolina.[26] South Carolina granted divorces between 1872 and 1878, but prohibited divorces after that time until the mid-twentieth century.

Bertram Wyatt-Brown suggests that when the only legal options available to prosecute adultery were a criminal conversation suit or a divorce petition, for a man to avail himself

---

[24] Thomas Buckley, *The Great Catastrophe of My Life: Divorce in the Old Dominion* (Chapel Hill: University of North Carolina Press, 2002) 56–65.

[25] Stoney Creek Independent Presbyterian Church, Prince William's Parish, SC, *Covenant and Confession*, "Of Marriages."

[26] Phillips, *Putting Asunder*, 153–57, 445–48.

of either meant sacrificing his honor by exposing his marital failures. Whether out of shame, convictions, or inconvenience, divorce was rare in the South. Although most Southern states transferred divorce jurisdiction from legislatures to courts in 1820s, divorce statistics remained considerably low. How then was a spouse to respond to adultery? Society recommended that offended husbands take the law into their own hands, informally punishing their unfaithful wives and their partners as they saw fit. Offended wives, however, were expected to keep the matter silent out of respect for the family's honor.[27]

The moral economy found in church discipline in some ways complements and in other ways contradicts that of Southern society. Early fornication laws assigned punishment for men and women alike. In practice, fornication was often overlooked or accepted in men. Likewise, adultery came to be seen as trivial or even fashionable in some circles, particularly for men. Women were often expected to hold their peace, and men had to do likewise to hide their shame or defend their honor with manly vengeance. Divorce was rare in the South, but the only double standard in the matter is one of class rather than gender. When divorce could only be obtained by individual acts of the legislature, only the wealthy could take advantage of the loophole. Ironically, as will be seen, it was those at the bottom of the social ladder that opened a loophole for the acceptance of divorce in churches. But in matters of divorce, church discipline was enforced with considerable equality and consistency.

Likely assumed a precursor to sexual promiscuity, excessive flirting also was taken seriously by the churches. Wheeley's, finding their relationship to be a "bad example," censured a woman in 1802 for whispering and keeping company with a

[27] Bertram Wyatt-Brown, *Honor and Violence in the Old South*, 100–105.

young man. The woman was obstinate, however, and was excommunicated the following year. Turkey Creek censured a man in 1813 for "going with a young man to steal a man's daughter." In 1807, a Brier Creek male slave was charged with being "too grate [flirtatious] with women." The Tyger records include three examples of white men being examined for the same fault. In 1803, one man was judged to be "acting contrary to Christian order by pushing for a familiarity with a woman." Finding the charge "authenticated by his own hand writing and acknowledged to in part," the church excommunicated him promptly. The following year, a man and woman of the same last name were accused of "unseemly familiarity." The details of that case are unclear. They may or may not have been married, but whatever the case, the church concluded that the accusations were nothing more than "groundless jealousies." Before the month was over, however, the same man was accused of whoredom in a scandalous case, the records of which are rich in detail.

Another male member and his daughters accused David Forester[28] of being too familiar with a neighbor woman, and on one occasion attempting to seduce one of the daughters. Forrest confessed that his behavior had been "lightminded," and the church decided to "lay restrictions on him to avoid the light mindedness he confessed he was guilty of." But in 1811, the man was again allegedly seen in secret with a woman. When questioned by several brethren, Forrest at first refused to answer the charges but then acknowledged the story was true with the exception of minor details. He later appeared on trial before the church, claiming that he had gotten lost on a path and accidentally found himself at the plantation he intended to avoid. Then two brethren objected, denying that the said path

[28] The spelling "Forrest" is also used.

existed. When the church pointed out this and other contradictions, he accused the church of "picking and criticizing and dealing hard with him." The record book states, "from these contradictions and many more with many suspicious circumstances the church found [him] in disorder and unanimously agree[d] to his excommunication."

Fornication may have been socially acceptable, at least for men, but just as fighting and gambling, it struck Southern churchgoers as a more serious matter. Eighteenth-century church records described fornication with words such as "whoredom" and "uncleanness." David Turner observes in *Fashioning Adultery* that "hard names" such as "adultery," "whoredom," or "uncleanness" were commonly used in England prior to the simultaneous rise of "civility" and tolerance of adultery, when softer words such as "gallantry" and "cuckoldry" came into vogue.[29] In instances where the suspected offenders were living together, churches described the offense by its circumstances: "keeping house." Tyger charged a woman in 1811 with "keeping a single man's house." And in 1801, Jersey excommunicated a woman for "living with a man in an unlawful way." First Corinthians deals at length with the sin of fornication. The Apostle Paul instructed churches to "purge out" members guilty of such offenses.[30]

---

[29] David Turner, *Fashioning Adultery: Gender, Sex, and Civility in England, 1660–1740* (New York: Cambridge University Press, 2002) 26, 35, 45. The Adultery Act of 1650 made the crime punishable by death, but during the Restoration period, church courts lost influence and adultery, if it followed certain rules of civility, became increasingly "fashionable."

[30] Paul continued, "But now I have written unto you not to keep company, if any man that is called a brother be a fornicator, or covetous, or an idolater, or a railer, or a drunkard, or an extortioner; with such an one no not to eat. For what have I to do to judge them also that are

Although most discipline cases involving fornication and adultery are lacking in detail, records do reveal important patterns in how churches dealt with male and female members. Two women were excommunicated for "uncleanness," one in Brier Creek (1786), and one in Eaton's (1775). Three women were excommunicated for "whoredom," one in Jersey (1805), one in Brier Creek (1806), and one in Clear Spring (1808). Poplar Spring excommunicated a woman in 1794 for "being with a man as man and wife before marriage." First Woodruff excommunicated a woman in 1796 for being too familiar with a man before marriage. Turkey Creek dealt with similar cases in 1786 and 1807. In 1786, Sarah Smith was excommunicated for "suffering a young man to bed with her daughter in her own house and also for beding with a man herself in his own house," but she was soon after restored to fellowship. In 1807, the church suspended Nancy Posey for "going to Mr. Edmund Ware's and suffering a married man to come and lie on the bed with her." She contradicted herself in her defense, and compounded the charge with her "railing," "speaking unadvisedly," having a "hard spirit," and refusing to keep silence according to the moderator's instructions. She was quickly restored to fellowship "with reproof and instruction," but only a month later she was again

---

without? do not ye judge them that are within? But them that are without God judgeth. Therefore put away from among yourselves that wicked person.... Know ye not that your bodies are the members of Christ? shall I then take the members of Christ, and make them the members of an harlot? God forbid.... Flee fornication. Every sin that a man doeth is without the body; but he that committeth fornication sinneth against his own body.... It is good for a man not to touch a woman. Nevertheless, to avoid fornication, let every man have his own wife, and let every woman have her own husband...if they cannot contain, let them marry: for it is better to marry than to burn" (1 Cor 5:11-13; 6:15, 18; 7:1-2, 9).

accused of "unbecoming conduct with a certain Mr. Gray from Kentucky." This time she was excommunicated, and the church immediately turned its attention to Mary Posey, possibly Nancy's daughter, for "renting herself from the church" and making a "scandalous" and "groundless" report against a sister of the church. She too was excommunicated.

Eaton's excommunicated a male slave for "uncleanness" in 1793, and Reedy River excommunicated a male slave in 1801 for "whoredom." But women and black men do not appear to have been over-represented in such discipline cases. A man of Lick Fork made recantation in 1811 for "being too intimate with a base young woman." One white man of Tyger who was charged with uncleanness by a woman in 1805 does not appear to have been excommunicated after witnesses (white and black) were cited to give testimony. Perhaps there was a lack of evidence to substantiate the charge. Whatever the case, other white men were excommunicated for this type of charge. In 1792 Poplar Spring excommunicated an "Esquire" for uncleanness, and in 1777 Sandy Creek excommunicated a man for "uncleanness with his negro wench." Ashley River suspended a man in 1753 for living in fornication, and eventually excluded him in 1755 for living in adultery. In 1762, Welsh Neck suspended a married couple for being convicted of "criminal conversation" before their marriage. Both husband and wife were restored to fellowship within months, after demonstrating their repentance to the satisfaction of the church.[31]

Not surprisingly, several discipline cases involved illegitimate children. Just as the Anglican Church, Baptist churches in the Carolinas refused to ignore the sin of illegitimacy among their members. It is clear though that they handled such cases, in

[31] Terms such as "fornication" and "criminal conversation" are sometimes used for both fornication and adultery.

harmony with their doctrine, with a combination of "law" and "grace." The Apostle Paul wrote that "the law was our schoolmaster to bring us unto Christ, that we might be justified by faith" (Gal 3:24). These churches used the force of biblical "law" to convict members who were guilty of sins such as illegitimacy, but once offenders acknowledged the sin and demonstrated repentance, they could expect to meet with the "grace" of forgiveness.

There were twelve cases of women being excommunicated for having "base borne children,"[32] being found pregnant "in a single state of life," and similar charges.[33] Of the two women excommunicated by Tyger in 1811, one was reported by her own father, and the other's father disapproved of the proceedings against his daughter. The woman Skewarkey excommunicated in 1807 was cited by her father, who also served as moderator in business meetings, and the woman excommunicated in 1808 was cited by a woman. The woman from Jersey was excommunicated on "evidence from Caintuck," which followed her to her new home. Lick Fork excommunicated a female slave in 1794 for "having children without a husband." Wheeley's censured a slave girl in 1801 for the same offense. She claimed she had "always looked upon [the father] as her husband," but the

---

[32] See Norman Eliason, *Tarheel Talk: An Historical Study of the English Language in North Carolina to 1860* (Chapel Hill: University of North Carolina Press, 1956) 162, 188, 259. The terms "base-born child," "base-begotten child," and "natural son" were commonly used in place of "illegitimate child." According to Eliason, "base-born" was still used occasionally in western North Carolina when he published his book. See also pp. 44–49 for his discussion of church record books as linguistic evidence.

[33] Reedy River 1818, Tyger 1811 (2), Skewarkey 1807/1808, Jersey 1806, Sandy Creek 1808, 1809, 1816, and 1821, Lick Fork 1794, Wheeley's 1801.

church found cause for doubt since the two had been apart for years. The church concluded that she had sinned by failing to consult either her mistress or the church, but "suffered herself to be destroyed by [the child's father], under promise of living with her as a husband."

But unwed mothers were not always excommunicated, and fathers did not always go unpunished.[34] A Skewarkey woman who confessed her fault in 1788 gave satisfaction to the church and remained in fellowship. Part of the explanation for the low number of excommunicated unwed fathers may be the elusive nature of evidence against them, but another likely factor is the low rate of church membership among young men.[35] A church could only discipline a man who was a member; if only the mother was a member, then the church could only exercise formal discipline against her. Such explanations only go so far, though. If there were no discipline cases involving unwed fathers, one would suspect the existence of a double standard. But such is not the case. Another church accused a Brier Creek man of having a child "sworn" to him in 1820. He confessed the charge was true and was promptly excommunicated. Two years later, a Sandy Creek man had a child "laid at his door," and was excommunicated for disregarding church authority when cited.

Lick Fork also dealt with two breach of promise cases in the 1790s. In 1792, a sister got "out of temper" with a brother about his "disappointing her daughter in marriage." Both members

---

[34] Lindman says illegitimacy was overwhelmingly the fault of women, and that "White men suffered accusations for sexual misconduct such as adultery, but they were never cited for illegitimacy, and only occasionally for premarital and extramarital sexual activity" (*A World of Baptists*, 221–22).

[35] See Patricia Bonomi, *Under the Cope of Heaven: Religion, Society, and Politics in Colonial America* (New York: Oxford University Press, 1986) 112.

were censured briefly before being restored to fellowship upon their repentance. In 1795, the same man appears to have again been censured for breach of promise. He was charged with "playing with and kissing a young woman and for speaking things not true and for trying to deceive a woman after promiseing her marriage and for visiting [a certain home] more than be come a married man."

These churches clearly valued matrimony, but it was not enough simply to enter into a marriage. Churches were also concerned with maintaining harmony between spouses.[36] Disputes between couples usually resulted in arbitration rather than excommunication. Bear Creek was successful in settling a disorder between a couple in 1799. A Reedy River woman was reconciled to her husband to the satisfaction of the church in 1816. An Eaton's woman was charged with using "unbecoming discourse" towards her husband in 1783 but gave satisfaction and was retained in fellowship. The outcome of couple disputes was not always satisfactory. In 1810, a Tyger man "laid in a distress which had taken place between him and his wife." The church, considering it a private matter, delegated a presbytery including several sisters of the church to look into the matter on a Saturday. After investigation, the delegation convinced the church that the husband and wife should both be excommunicated.

---

[36] See Daniel Blake Smith, *Inside the Great House: Planter Family Life in Eighteenth-Century Chesapeake Society* (Ithaca: Cornell University Press, 1980) and Jan Lewis, *The Pursuit of Happiness: Family and Values in Jefferson's Virginia* (Cambridge: Cambridge University Press, 1983) on "companionate marriage."

Skewarkey was plagued by several couple disputes. In 1792, a husband was cited for "quareling with another man and spiting in his face and saying if he was able he would fight him." Further investigation revealed that the husband was reacting to insulting abuse toward his wife. The church, considering it "a very trying case," admonished both husband and wife "for not behaving in Christian like manner" and let the matter go. In 1796, a committee was unable to effect reconciliation between a couple, resulting in the excommunication of both the following year. In 1802, a woman made an accusation against a man of the same last name (likely her husband), but after long debate the church threw out the case for lack of evidence. In 1808, the church heard a husband's charge against his wife but ruled in her favor and retained both as members. The same year, the church ruled in a wife's favor in a case involving a couple's "misunderstanding," this time excommunicating the husband after a committee failed to effect his reconciliation. The following year, the couple that had been retained in fellowship was once again involved in a dispute, and this time both were excommunicated. In 1814–1815, another couple experienced an "unhappy difference," and both were excommunicated at the recommendation of a committee. Records of couple disputes rarely offer detailed information about the nature of the conflict, but there are exceptions. In 1808, for example, Turkey Creek excommunicated a man for "taking a young woman in his chair and carrying her into Greenville against his wife's will also for saying he had lost all affection for her."

Discipline cases occasionally involved wife abuse. E. P. Thompson describes the tradition among England's plebeians of regulating such behavior with "rough music."[37] This practice, by

[37] "Rough music" referred to the procession of masked young men who carried pans, bells, or other loud noisemakers past the wrongdoer's house with the intent of causing long-lasting humiliation. In addition to

humiliating and punishing neighbors who broke the rules of acceptable behavior, was one way for a community to enforce its moral economy.[38] Baptist churches, however, did so by means of church discipline. In 1738, Ashley River suspended a male slave for beating his wife. A Jersey man accused of drinking too much and abusing his wife in 1792 acknowledged his transgression and requested the church's patience with him. He was eventually excommunicated in 1794. A Tyger man attempted to justify himself for whipping his wife in 1804. The church disagreed and condemned his behavior, but it is unclear whether formal action was ever taken against him. In 1805–1806, Brier Creek excommunicated a man for beating his wife and failing to appear when cited. In 1821, a man answered reports that he had abused his wife, confessing that he had gotten angry and said things he should not have, but proving to the satisfaction of the church that he was not guilty of physical abuse.[39] Lick Fork considered two cases of wife abuse in 1805. One man was censured and restored, but the other was excommunicated.

Cases of abuse were not limited to wife beating. Bush River excommunicated a man in 1804 for assaulting a woman, a charge that turned out to be false. Lick Fork censured a man in 1795 for "beating a young woman that lived with him." In an unusual case of 1811, Turkey Creek excommunicated a woman for abusing her husband and brother-in-law both verbally and physically. The notorious Nancy Robartson had already been disciplined for participation in horse racing, dancing, and

---

the cacophony, the procession might have re enacted the offense, hurled insults, or recited rude poems. Effigies of the accused were often then burned or tossed into a pond or river for a "ritual drowning."

[38] Thompson, "The Moral Economy," 493, 505, 523.

[39] According to Lindman, men were chastised for the rare accusations of abusing or deserting their families (*A World of Baptists*, 222).

speaking out of order. She was then charged with "calling her husband a dam'd lyar, also for calling her brotherinlaw a [crude name denigrating his mother]." In addition, "when she return'd home from meeting threating to strike her husband in the mouth also struck her husband and broke his gun." Such relationships could not be tolerated in the church membership, whether the aggressor was a husband or a wife.

Another concern was separation. The Apostle Paul commanded husbands and wives, "Defraud ye not one the other, except it be with consent for a time, that ye may give yourselves to fasting and prayer; and come together again, that Satan tempt you not for your incontinency." He continued, "And unto the married I command, yet not I, but the Lord, Let not the wife depart from her husband: But and if she depart, let her remain unmarried, or be reconciled to her husband: and let not the husband put away his wife" (1 Cor 7:5, 10-11). In the American South, throughout most of the eighteenth-century county courts were authorized to grant only "separations," which legally disentangled a couple's property rights and gave each spouse permission to live apart, but not to remarry during the lifetime of the other.[40]

Just as county courts demanded that applicants for a legal separation agreement produce just cause, churches also expected a good explanation. In 1760, Welsh Neck inquired as to why a wife was not living with her husband, but no action seems to have been taken against her. In 1763, the same church suspended a woman for living in willful separation from her husband, but after sending messengers of care to her, the church restored her to fellowship the following year. A Sandy Creek woman left her husband in 1817 but was retained in fellowship. Women who

[40] Buckley, *The Great Catastrophe of My Life*, 26; Phillips, *Putting Asunder*, 143.

left their husbands sometimes gave churches satisfactory reason for doing so. A Lick Fork query of 1798, for example, agreed that it was permissible for a woman to leave her husband in cases of fornication.

Other women failed to satisfy church inquiries. A Jersey woman left her husband in 1798. Her perplexed church sent a query to its association the following year asking, "What shall be done with a woman in the church that refuses to live with her husband and refuses to give a reason for not living with him[?]" The association recommended that the church hold a meeting with the spouses present and to ask sister churches for help if necessary. After another attempt to reconcile her, she "still refused subjection to the church or her husband," and was "for her great offenses excommunicated." In 1804, another woman of the church left her husband and was excommunicated by choice.

Although it was less common for men to leave their wives, men who did were held accountable for their actions. First Woodruff excommunicated a male member in 1805 for not living with his wife. Clear Springs excommunicated a white man in 1818, and Brier Creek excommunicated a black man in 1799, both for leaving their wives. Roaring River even held parents accountable for their behavior concerning the separation of their children. In 1785 Charles Cates informed the church "of his management concerning his son and wife parting." At the same time, the church cited Gibson Maner to "satisfie the church of his behavour concerning his Daughter and her husband parting."

Although Southern society was more permissive of adulterers than adulteresses, churches consistently penalized both. Society may have expected wives to keep their unfaithful husbands' secrets, but such was not the case in church discipline. As with other charges, adultery cases did not always lead to a member's excommunication. Two members of Tyger were accused of adultery in 1808, but the church concluded that the accusation was false. Ashley River considered excommunicating a man for adultery in 1747, but decided to reduce his penalty to suspension. A few years later, that man was restored to fellowship upon his repentance. In 1753, the church suspended another man for adultery, but after he continued to live in that state for a couple years, he was finally excommunicated for continuing to live in adultery.

In 1807, a Reedy River man charged a woman with falsehood, and she charged him with "attempting her honor at many different times." Apparently, he was denying her accusation that he had made repeated sexual advances. After hearing witnesses on both sides, the woman was cleared and the man requested that a committee see if his wife had anything to say about his accuser and her husband. The man, a colonel, was excommunicated. White men were also excommunicated for adultery by Bush River in 1805, by Poplar Spring in 1807 and 1820, by Skewarkey in 1803, by Sandy Run in 1785, and by Jersey in 1803. White women were excommunicated for the same offense by Welsh Neck in 1788, Skewarkey in 1797, Bear Creek in 1801, Boiling Springs in 1812, and by Jersey in 1804, 1810, and 1811. Reedy River excommunicated a black man for adultery in 1806, and Brier Creek excommunicated "Servant Hal" in 1821. Bush River excommunicated a male slave in 1805 and a female slave in 1811 for adultery. In 1792, Sandy Creek excommunicated a black man and a black woman belonging to different masters, and Jersey excommunicated a black woman in 1810. Lick Fork excommunicated a male slave for "leaving his wife and taking up with another woman" in 1815. In cases of adulterous ministers, censure went beyond excommunication. In 1805 Bush River stated in a query that it was unscriptural "to attend on the preaching of a minister who has been excluded for the sin of adultery or other crimes."

To charge a person with fornication or adultery was a serious matter, and false accusations were punished with as much rigor as adultery itself. One example is that of the Bush

River preacher who was excommunicated in 1805 for claiming to have had an affair with a woman of the church prior to their becoming members. Another example is found in the case of the Lick Fork man who in 1816 confessed to having been intoxicated when he falsely accused a sister of being pregnant. This is also evident in Reedy River's scandalous case involving Brother Blackwell.

In October 1805, another church made allegations against Blackwell. In November, he acknowledged the charge in part but denied drinking too much and questioning a woman about her faithfulness to her husband. He acknowledged that he was guilty of "light mindedness" but denied meaning any harm. That satisfied the majority of Reedy River, but some members of the other church kept the case alive the following year. New charges and evidence surfaced. Blackwell allegedly drank too much and accused the same woman of bearing an illegitimate child, along with other "blackguardish conversation." Blackwell was also accused of getting drunk on other occasions and missing a church meeting while going after more liquor on his horse. When he appeared before the church and heard the latest charges against him, he "flew in a violent passion and forsook the church, for which conduct together with the charges he was excommunicated." Then in March 1810, Blackwell "made recantation" of his crime and was restored to fellowship before being granted a letter of dismissal to another church. In May, the church reconsidered whether it had restored him on proper grounds. The church clerk was questioned for giving Blackwell his letter after two other brothers asked him to withhold it. In June, the church decided to forgive the clerk but to excommunicate Blackwell once again, determining that "whenever we hear where he is we write to let him know his standing."

Divorce was not a scriptural option with which to respond to adultery, but husbands and wives both had a means of holding an unfaithful spouse accountable by bringing the matter before the church. Churches refused to sanction remarriage, as evidenced by queries and several discipline cases. In 1796 Shoal Creek proclaimed that it was not lawful to receive "a mail member in to fellow ship who while in natures darkness maries a wife and after some time his wife forsook him and took up with a nother man and livs with him in the sin of adultrey in consequins of which he married a second wife after which he professes to be renewed by the Spirit of God." Turkey Creek agreed in 1802 that it was not permissible "to receive a member into full fellowship that has been married twice and both living."

In 1808, Turkey Creek excommunicated a man for "marrying a second wife while the first was liveing." Sandy Creek excommunicated a man in 1784 for marrying another man's wife, and Reedy River excommunicated another man for his second marriage in 1801. According to Benedict, Welsh Neck pastor Nicholas Bedgegood

> left a wife in England when he came to America, and after he had been pastor of the Welsh-Neck church a number of years, he married another, and alleged in justification of his conduct, that his first wife would not come after him to America, and that he had been informed of her death before his second marriage. His brethren were by no means satisfied with this statement, but requested him to attend the Association, and give them a more full and satisfactory explanation of his conduct. To this summons he did not attend, and was, therefore, disowned.[41]

Women were occasionally excommunicated for remarriage too. In 1795, Welsh Neck excommunicated a woman for marrying a man whose wife was living. And in 1816 Lick Fork considered an interesting case of a first husband's questionable death. The records read, "Rebecca has married the second

---

[41] David Benedict, *A General History of the Baptist Denomination in America*, vol. 2 (Boston: Lincoln & Edmands, 1813) 133.

Husband believing the first to be dead but reports made the matter uncertain which caused part of the church to reject her untill the last Husband died then they want the first to receive her."

Although slave marriages were not legally recognized in the South, churches respected them as valid. The Kehukee Association answered the following queries in 1778: "Is the marriage of servants lawful before God, which is not complied with according to the laws of the land? Answer: Yes. Is it duty to hold a member in fellowship who breaks the marriage of servants? Answer: No."[42] Churches also held slaves to the standard of lifelong marriage. In 1739 Ashley River excommunicated a male slave for "seeking after another wife, while his lawful one was yet living." In 1809 Bush River charged a female slave with leaving her husband "and taking up with another man." And in 1803, Wheeleys excommunicated a slave woman for "marrying when her former husband was yet alive & in reach of her."

These rulings were consistent with the doctrine of marital indissolubility, but matters became complicated when some churches considered the circumstances of forced separations due to the slave trade. Baptist churches recognized slave marriages as valid and disapproved of masters who separated slave couples. But when such forced separations occurred, churches

---

[42] It appears that the Kehukee Association continued to hold to the doctrine of marital indissolubility. Hassell and Hassell's history laments the nineteenth century's "gradual but steady decay of the appreciation of the life-long sacredness of the marriage relation, the relaxation of the laws of divorce, and the alarming multiplication of divorces and of 'consecutive polygamy' (the New England States of the Union occupying a miserable pre-eminence, and Protestant countries far surpassing Roman Catholic countries, in this corrupting disregard of the Divine law of marriage" (*History of the Church of God* (1886; repr., Ellenwood GA: Old School Hymnal Co., 1983) 829, 581.

disagreed over whether it was permissible for slaves to remarry.[43] Thomas Buckley has pointed out the ironic role of slavery in undermining the indissolubility of marriage in Virginia; when churches considered the pitiful plight of slaves whose marriages had been broken by the cruel slave trade, they bent the rules and began to condone remarriage.[44] Some Baptist

---

[43] For more on the relationship between black and white evangelicals in shaping Southern churches, see Mechal Sobel, *The World They Made Together: Black and White Values in Eighteenth-Century Virginia* (Princeton: Princeton University Press, 1989); Charles F. Irons, *The Origins of Proslavery Christianity: White and Black Evangelicals in Colonial and Antebellum Virginia* (Chapel Hill: University of North Carolina Press, 2008); Randolph Ferguson Scully, *Religion and the Making of Nat Turner's Virginia: Baptist Community and Conflict, 1740–1840* (Charlottesville: University of Virginia Press, 2008); Albert J. Raboteau, *Slave Religion: The "Invisible Institution" in the Antebellum South* (New York: Oxford University Press, 2004); and Sylvia R. Frey, *Come Shouting to Zion: African-American Protestantism in the American South and British Caribbean to 1830* (Chapel Hill: The University of North Carolina Press, 1998). For more on the origins of slavery in the South and the complex relationship between masters and slaves, see Betty Wood, *The Origins of American Slavery: Freedom and Bondage in the English Colonies* (New York: Hill and Wang, 1998); Peter H. Wood, *Black Majority: Negroes in Colonial South Carolina from 1670 through the Stono Rebellion* (New York: W. W. Norton & Company, 1996), and Robert Olwell, *Masters, Slaves, and Subjects: The Culture of Power in the South Carolina Low Country, 1740–1790* (Ithaca: Cornell University Press, 1998). Emily West recognizes slave marriages as a form of resistance to oppression of slavery in *Chains of Love: Slave Couples in Antebellum South Carolina* (Champaign: University of Illinois Press, 2004). David Silkenat highlights the role of black Southerners in the further erosion of divorce's stigma following the Civil War in *Moments of Despair: Suicide, Divorce, and Debt in Civil War Era North Carolina* (Chapel Hill: University of North Carolina Press, 2011).

[44] Buckley, *The Great Catastrophe of My Life*, 65–68.

churches followed the example of Presbyterians in doing so, but others resisted the change. Of the churches surveyed in this study, only those in Up Country South Carolina appear to have begun following the new trend of allowing slave remarriage in the early nineteenth century. Keep in mind that South Carolina refused to grant divorces throughout this period.[45] The churches that began tolerating remarriage apparently had prospective members who had obtained divorces in other states, or in the case of slaves, were never legally married to begin with.[46]

---

[45] North Carolina was slightly more flexible. "An Act to restrain all married Persons from marrying again whilst their former Wives or former Husbands are living" (North Carolina Sessions Laws, 1790, chap. 11, microfiche, North Carolina Division of Archives and History, Raleigh NC). This law allowed remarriage in cases of desertion "beyond the sea" for at least seven years, presumably to accommodate Tories following the American Revolution. Special thanks to Cindy Kierner for sharing this reference after listening to my presentation at the Southern Association for Women Historians conference in 2009.

[46] Lindman saw no evidence of exceptions for slavery's circumstances in Virginia: "Regardless of status or circumstance, black members were expected to follow white notions of proper sexual behavior or suffer discipline for their deviance. An offense specific to the black experience was leaving a "lawful" spouse and taking up with another. As enslaved people, many slave men and women constituted relationships considered informal or illegal by whites. The constraints of slavery made abroad marriages and serial monogamy two options for blacks who desired marital relationships. Black men and women alike were cited, excluded, and excommunicated for what were defined as irregular marriages according to white members.... The consequences of slavery led many blacks over time to form multiple unions. This behavior, however, was not approved of by the white church leaders, and white Baptists displayed little sensitivity to the disruptions of black family life caused by slavery. The Baptist moral code as defined by whites in the church circumscribed black activity while at the same time

At the turn of the century, a Reedy River man confessed to the church that he had married a woman whose first husband was still living. The majority decided that they had been wrong to receive him as a member, but after asking for advice from the association it appears that the church retained him. In 1801, the church excommunicated a man for remarrying. And as late as 1813, a man was examined for allegedly having a hand in initiating a bill of divorce for a couple that was about to pass. But the church's position against remarriage had shown signs of weakness when in May 1805 an adultery charge against a black man set off a year-long debate over the remarriage of black members. In August, the church "took into consideration the marriage of black people whether they shall marry a second wife or husband being forcefully separated from the former and they still living and concluded it is not pointedly agreeable to scripture but some being in favour to tolerate it is continued for further consideration." The matter was repeatedly laid over until in May 1806, when the church determined that

> considering the unhappy circumstance of their separation from wives and husbands by their cruel owners when not a voluntary act of the Blacks but torn by violent tyranny like bone from bone their marrying a second time appears to be one of the cruel consequences of slavery we far from saying it is right know not what better to do than bear our burdens in some extreme cases but should always rather they would abstain from marrying in that way. Further that it be a matter of dealing of censure if they marry without first making it known to the church.

In 1804 Clear Springs answered a query concerning the remarriage of blacks with less uncertainty: "May a slave who is forced from his wife in a distant land and brought to this

---

ignoring the everyday trials of life in bondage" (*A World of Baptists*, 211–12).

country take another wife[?] Answer we think he may." Not surprisingly, churches began to bend the remarriage rules for white members as well. When Tyger took up a query in 1801 whether there was "scriptural toleration for a man to put away his wife for any cause and marry another," instead of offering a conclusive answer one way or the other, the church postponed its judgment indefinitely. In 1811, when investigating the standing of a woman with two husbands, the church determined that she appeared to be living with her lawful one. The circumstances of this case are uncertain, but it seems likely that the church had begun to consider second marriages lawful, even during the lifetime of the previous spouse. It is likely that churches outside Up Country South Carolina began to bend the rules around the turn of the century as well, by overlooking the offense rather than explicitly condoning it. It is also possible that churches such as Welsh Neck, which authorized a separate black congregation for a time, found such an arrangement a convenient way to transfer the responsibility for regulating slave marriages to the slaves themselves.[47]

It is ironic that slavery, linked by some with marital "oppression," actually forced change upon the institution of marriage. Scriptural marriage was seen as beneficial to both husbands and wives, and both were expected to honor their respective vows. It is unlikely that many slaves saw their subordinate position in a positive light, but many wives, not viewing themselves as slaves, did have a positive view of their positions as women. Just as other types of discipline cases under consideration, those involving fornication, marital conflict, and adultery fail to support the double-standard oppression thesis. Instead, the pattern followed by these churches in disciplinary

[47] Heyrman dates the segregation of worship services to the decades following the Revolution (*Southern Cross: The Beginnings of the Bible Belt* [Chapel Hill: University of North Carolina Press, 1997] 67–68).

action suggests that, although women were undoubtedly ascribed a position of "subjection" to men (for example, by remaining silent in the assembly), they also enjoyed a surprising degree of fairness. Church discipline was often found protecting their interests against the abuses of men. Perhaps this explains in part why few of these women appeared to resent their "subjection" or equate it with "oppression."

CONCLUSION

Meeting Adjourned

In the past couple decades, a few historians have ventured into the world of Baptist church record books, sitting in on business meetings of past centuries by way of archival research. In *The Enclosed Garden: Women and Community in the Evangelical South, 1830–1900*, Jean Friedman examined a few nineteenth-century churches in North Carolina and Georgia.[1] Monica Najar explored churches scattered throughout North Carolina, Virginia, Tennessee, and Kentucky in her dissertation, *Evangelizing the South: Gender, Race, and Politics in the Early Evangelical South, 1765–1850*.[2] Greg Wills became well acquainted with a large sample of Georgia churches in *Democratic Religion: Freedom, Authority, and Church Discipline in the Baptist South, 1785–1900*.[3]

---

[1] Whether Friedman's sample of records should be taken as representative of Southern churches is highly questionable. She focuses on six Baptist churches, two in North Carolina and four in Georgia. She also refers occasionally to nine North Carolina churches in a study conducted by C.V. Smith (*The Enclosed Garden: Women and Community in the Evangelical South, 1830–1900* [Chapel Hill: University of North Carolina Press, 1985]).

[2] Monica Najar, *Evangelizing the South: Gender, Race, and Politics in the Early Evangelical South, 1765–1850* (Madison: University of Wisconsin, 2000). Published more recently is Monica Najar, *Evangelizing the South: A Social History of Church and State in Early America* (New York: Oxford University Press, 2008).

[3] Greg Wills, *Democratic Religion: Freedom, Authority, and Church Discipline in the Baptist South, 1785–1900* (New York: Oxford University Press, 1997).

Each of these historians walked away from their encounters with a different perspective of Baptist church discipline.

Jean Friedman took a negative view of gender equality in church discipline, arguing that it followed a double standard to support the Southern social order.[4] As other historians have done with an earlier period, Friedman claims to have found evidence of a double standard in church discipline during the nineteenth century. Her tables suggest that three times as many men were accused in church trials as women and that men were usually charged with lesser offenses of misconduct such as drinking, dancing, and disorder. Women, on the other hand, were accused of more serious sexual offenses such as fornication and adultery at a considerably higher rate. Furthermore, men were twice as likely to receive forgiveness. According to Friedman, that more men were accused and forgiven proves that they were expected to fail and were treated with greater leniency. That sexual offenses were taken more seriously she interprets as proof of a double standard. And that fewer women bothered to petition for restoration she takes to mean that women lacked confidence that they would succeed although she does point out examples of female audacity in church proceedings against them.[5]

Such conclusions are largely based on perspective. Could we not just as easily conclude that more men were charged with lesser offenses because they were under closer scrutiny? That women were charged in smaller numbers with greater offenses

---

[4] She argues, "The male-dominated [church] trials all but excluded women from the proceedings.... Women did not vote in the evangelical church trials although they were present in the congregation during the hearings," but then admits that some churches allowed women to vote and that women were frequently seen challenging the "rule of silence" (Friedman, *The Enclosed Garden*, 13–14).

[5] Ibid., 15, Appendix.

because lesser misconduct was overlooked? Remember that women often outnumbered men in the church. Friedman's tables show that few members charged with sexual offenses were restored, male or female. Is this proof of a double standard? The burden of repentance fell on the offender; if he or she refused to acknowledge the crime and demonstrate repentance, a church had every right to deny restoration of fellowship. My research in eighteenth and early nineteenth-century church records calls into question Friedman's assumptions about the nature of church discipline in the Carolinas. If inequality did change over the course of the nineteenth century, church records should reflect the transformation, but I suspect that a balanced interpretation of the records would confirm that the moral economy found in Southern churches continued to represent the interests of both men and women into the nineteenth century.

Unlike Friedman, Najar recognizes the positive aspect of church discipline. Churches, she argues, challenged the social order by intruding into the private realm and regulating marriages in ways that sometimes clashed with the authority of husbands. Interpreting marriage as a partnership with mutual obligations and interdependence, they policed discord, abuse, and property rights in a way that often sided with wives. Najar's acknowledgment that church discipline challenged the inequality of social mores resembles my interpretation; however, churches' success in evangelizing the South should not be overstated. As Najar states, church authority extended only to those who voluntarily subjected themselves to it. One must ask whether the South was evangelized or whether evangelicals were Southernized. As Heyrman has argued, churches had to accommodate the Southern social order before gaining significant influence. Heyrman makes a valid point about the fact of accommodation; it is concerning the nature of that accommodation that we disagree. Baptist churches accommodated society not by enforcing a double standard but by abandoning their standards over time.

Wills also takes a positive view of church discipline. He recognizes that the authoritarianism seen in discipline served a respectable purpose: maintenance of orthodoxy and purity. Discipline's exclusivism served to separate church from world. And although it did support a form of social hierarchy that distinguished between women and men, bonded and free, according to Wills, "women and blacks were at least as committed to the church's pruning knife as white men were." Unlike Najar, however, Wills emphasizes not church discipline's success in reforming the world but its demise as a result of compromising with the world. After the Civil War, he argues, "Baptist observers began to lament that church discipline was foundering, and it was." Growing churches became increasingly reluctant to cut their numbers. When, for example, young converts refused to give up dancing, churches began to condone it. Wills points to toleration of dancing among youth as the most significant factor in discipline's overall decline. At one time, only Episcopalian churches found the practice acceptable. But during the nineteenth century the desire of youth to emulate the elite lifestyle, and the desire of churches to swell their ranks with the next generation, undermined one aspect of the moral economy and opened the door for disciplinary compromise in other areas. Wills observes, "Many Baptists shared a new vision of the church, replacing the pursuit of purity with the quest for efficiency. They lost the resolve to purge their churches of straying members…[discipline] simply faded away, as if Baptists had grown weary of holding one another accountable." Regulating the moral economy was a dirty, demanding job, and when wealthy influential members or crowds of new converts transgressed, it was especially tempting to sweep matters under the rug.[6]

Wills agrees with William Sweet that churches once served as "moral courts of the frontier," but he takes issue with those who equate church discipline with social control.[7] Wills reasons, "The faithful did not exercise discipline in order to constrain a wayward society. That was the task of families, communities, and governments. Churches disciplined to constrain confessing saints to good order and to preserve their purity. Church discipline was not about social control but about ecclesiastical control." Churches did effectively curb social disorder in their advocacy of temperance and Sabbatarianism. Wills continues, however,

> the more the churches concerned themselves with social order, the less they exerted church discipline.... As Baptists learned to reform the larger society, they forgot how they had once reformed themselves. Church discipline presupposed a stark dichotomy between the norms of society and the kingdom of God. The more evangelicals purified the society, the less they felt the urgency of a discipline that separated the church from the world.[8]

I concur wholeheartedly with Wills's interpretation of discipline's decline, but I date the beginning of that transition earlier in the nineteenth century. My own study of church records ends by 1830, a time of significant transition for the

---

[6] Discipline rates fell off sharply between 1840 and 1920, and by 1940 the excommunication rate had decreased 90 percent when compared to a century before. Membership rates, on the other hand, more than tripled in Baptist churches between the Civil War and the 1920s (Wills, *Democratic Religion*, 9, 116–26).

[7] William W. Sweet, "The Churches as Moral Courts of the Frontier," *Church History* 2 (1933): 3–21.

[8] Wills, *Democratic Religion*, 9–10.

Baptists of the South. My research into church discipline through the 1820s reveals that there was no great switch during the period wherein churches abandoned a position of gender equality for advocacy of an oppressive double standard. That does not mean, however, that the churches did not change at all. Southern evangelicals were not above changing over time and across space, but the subtle, complex changes seen in their moral economy during the nineteenth century demand cautious examination. I have chosen to conclude this study around the year 1830 because churches were then entering into a period of transition in many ways. Revivalism, doctrinal disputes, growth, organization, missions, denominational competition, and sectionalism all had an effect on the changing shape of Southern churches during this period. But to what extent, and in what ways, did changing times affect the subject at hand, the moral economy of church discipline?

In *Fifty Years Among the Baptists*, Baptist historian David Benedict reminisced about the changes he had witnessed among fellow Baptists over the first half of the nineteenth century. According to Benedict, changes in organization, doctrine, and discipline had been striking.[9] A major innovation in organization was the growth of Baptist associations and their transformation into missionary machines. The early associations were merely advisory bodies of church delegates. Church business, doctrinal or financial, remained in the hands of independent churches. It was not until 1814 that several Baptist leaders met in Philadelphia to create the General Missionary Convention.[10]

[9] David Benedict, *Fifty Years Among the Baptists* (New York: Sheldon & Co., 1860), cited in C. B. Hassell and S. Hassell, *History of the Church of God* (1886; repr., Ellenwood GA: Old School Hymnal Co., 1983) 751.

[10] This was also known as the "Triennial Convention" because it would meet every three years. After Adoniram Judson and Luther Rice

Breaking with the custom of early associations, in which each church funded its own (mostly domestic) missionary endeavors, the new convention oversaw the management of foreign missions. Doctrinally, the traditional Calvinism of many Baptists came under strain during the same period. American Baptists were traditionally Calvinistic, as can be seen in the widespread adoption of the Philadelphia Confession of Faith. But in the nineteenth century, they divided into "Gillite" and "Fullerite" camps, accusing each other of "Hyper-Calvinism" and "Arminianism," respectively.[11] Doctrinal deviation was especially apparent in new revivalist techniques. Prior to this period, instances of mass conversions were "few and far between" among Baptists, and "scarcely any of the new measures of more modern times were adopted."[12] But the new measures of Methodist revivalists did influence some Baptists, and these "revival ministers" rose in popularity, pleasing some with their results and causing others concern with their procedure.

Most Baptists, according to Benedict, overcame their doctrinal differences with compromise. He once said to a Free Will minister, "Your side has been coming up and ours has been

---

decided to become Baptists on their way to India as missionaries, they convinced these Baptists to form this organization to fund foreign missions.

[11] Andrew Fuller of England popularized the doctrine of a "general atonement" in many Baptist circles. Unlike John Gill, the English Baptist theologian of the previous century, Fuller taught that Christ died for everyone, and that individuals were responsible for applying the atonement personally. Gill believed in "limited atonement," the doctrine that Christ died only for the sins of those who were predestinated to salvation. According to Benedict, the "Fuller system" influenced many Baptist ministers to change their mode of addressing unconverted audiences, with insistent pleas that they come to God immediately.

[12] Benedict, *Fifty Years Among the Baptists*.

going down, till the chasm between the two parties is by no means so great as formerly." They also learned to compromise with other denominations. At the beginning of the nineteenth century, few Baptist churches even opened their pulpits to ministers of other denominations, but this too changed during the nineteenth century. For many Baptist churches, the distinction between Calvinist and Arminian, or between Baptist and non-Baptist was fading. Baptists were moving into the mainstream...or at least some of them were.

It was primarily disagreement over missionary endeavors that led to the split between "Old School" and "New School" Baptists across America around 1830, a split that was particularly sharp in the South. Decades before the Civil War divided brother against brother and North against South, the missions controversy divided the Kehukee Association of North Carolina and the Charleston Baptist Association of South Carolina. The Kehukee Association appointed Skewarkey's Pastor C. B. Hassell to write its history with the help of S. Hassell. Hassell and Hassell's history, published in 1886, details the experiences of the Kehukee Association in eastern North Carolina throughout the controversy that began early in the century. A majority of the association assented to experimenting with missionary endeavor in 1803, but by 1827 the association was prepared to abandon the enterprise. The problem was not with missionary activity itself, but with the controversial new methods of carrying it out cooperatively under the direction of associations instead of individual churches. When the association met in 1827, all thirty-five churches unanimously agreed to "Discard all Missionary Societies, Bible Societies and Theological Seminaries, and the practices heretofore resorted to for their support, in begging money from the public...believing these societies and institutions to be the inventions of men, and not warranted from the word of God."[13]

But the division of Baptists into Old and New School camps was more than simply a controversy over missionary activity. The differences between the Kehukee Baptist Association in North Carolina and the Charleston Association in South Carolina encapsulate an array of issues that divided Baptists of that time. In addition to modern missionary societies, the Kehukee Association also took issue in the same passage with the New School's approval of Freemasonry.[14] The Old School also criticized Temperance Societies. In contrast with the old moral economy's regulation by churches of members' drinking habits, these new societies were preaching the unorthodoxy of total abstinence from alcohol. New School Baptists seemed eager to join forces with all the innovations of the day. The New School also took pride in new educational endeavors such as Furman University in Greenville, South Carolina, and Wake Forest University in Winston-Salem, North Carolina. The Old School, in contrast, seemed to be stuck in the past. Looking back in 1886, Hassell and Hassell's history emphasized the extent to which Old and New School Baptists had gone their separate ways.

Members of the Kehukee Baptist Association believed their traditional moral economy was threatened by the innovations of the day. Comparable to the plebeians of E. P. Thompson's England, they were "rebellious in defense of custom." How,

---

[13] Hassell and Hassell, *History of the Church of God*.

[14] The Charleston Baptist Association had decided a query as early as 1798 by leaving individuals to decide for themselves whether they should join the secret society. The emphasis on Freemasonry in the Kehukee critique of the New School appears puzzling at first. To them it was a symbol of transferring loyalty from church to other organizations they saw as antithetical.

exactly, did the New School departure threaten the old moral economy of the churches? In the eyes of the Old School, the New School was abandoning tradition for the money-grubbing ways of the world. Church members and their financial contributions were being obtained in a manner inconsistent with the ways of the past. The New School plan for missions subverted the traditional method of carrying out God's work with tithes under the authority of autonomous churches. Individual duty was being overshadowed by corrupt collection agencies disguised as missionary societies. The Old School could not reconcile their moral economy with the emerging Christian capitalism. Doctrinal compromise with Arminian Baptists and other denominations was regarded as a clear violation of their subjection to God, an abandonment of their duty to uphold the true gospel. The family, too, appeared vulnerable to doctrinal declension, especially as more Southern churches made accommodations for divorce among their membership. New School compromises in doctrine and discipline seemed complicit in all the evils of the day.

Also troubling was the carnality infiltrating churches. Benedict noticed a change in his fifty years of observation:

> Fifty years ago it was contrary to Baptist rules for their members to seek such places of amusement as multitudes of them now resort to without any official censure or complaint. Our people then made a broad distinction between the church and the world, and if any of their members went over the line to the world's side, they were at once put under church discipline.

Hassell was troubled by the growing relationship between the church and the secular world, alleging that "the large unregenerate additions made to the membership...by Sunday Schools and galvanic revivals, have brought in numerous corruptions of doctrine and practice, so that there is scarcely the slightest difference between the professing church and the world."[15] The Scriptures that had guided the traditional moral economy warned churches against a close relationship with the secular world. Church members were not to be conformed to the world, and they could not serve both God and mammon. Since they were not of the world but had been called out of it, they should expect the world's hatred. The friend of the world was the enemy of God; a Christian could not love both.[16] But in the eyes of Old School Baptists, most churches of the nineteenth century were attempting to combine the old moral economy of individual subjection with a new one of collective dominance. The old moral economy would come under strain, and compromise would be inevitable.

A close relationship with the secular world also threatened unity among churches. Rachel Klein has shown that Regular Baptist churches such as Welsh Neck and Cashaway were composed of inland planters who identified more closely with the coastal elite than with the Up Country yeomanry. She credits these inland planters with overcoming sectional differences by solidifying the unity of coastal and inland slaveholders. As early as the 1760s, Regular Baptists were found among the South Carolina Regulators in a vigilante movement to bring law and order to the Up Country, while Separate Baptists to the west remained suspiciously detached from the movement. The concern of Regular Baptists with the maintenance of law and order included the social order that sanctioned slavery. Klein

---

[15] The Old School Baptists of North Carolina were not the only ones to offer such a critique. Hassell and Hassell cited writers from various denominations in England and America who shared their sentiments (*History of the Church of God* [1886; repr., Ellenwood GA: Old School Hymnal Co., 1983]).

[16] Rom 12:2; Matt 6:24; Luke 16:13; John 15, 17; James 4:4; 1 John 2.

estimates that 66 percent of Baptists were nonslaveholders, and that 90 percent of those lived in the Piedmont. Furthermore, perhaps as many as 40 percent of Baptist preachers were slaveholders in the late eighteenth century. As slavery spread and slaveholding and non-slaveholding Baptists negotiated their differences, religious influence tended to empower the planters."[17] In the 1830s, those Regular Baptists in the South who followed the New School became increasingly accommodating of slavery as they were caught up in the great sectional debate of their time.[18] Baptist leaders such as Richard Furman of Charleston busied themselves constructing a biblical defense of slavery, and many slaveholding pastors rallied enthusiastically around the Confederate flag. New School Baptists of the North and South, along with Presbyterians and Methodists, divided over the issue of slavery prior to the Civil War. But according to

---

[17] "Of the 120 known South Carolina Regulators," Klein writes, "the only identifiable Baptists belonged to the Regular churches of Welsh Neck and Cashaway." Among them were Evan Pugh (Cashaway pastor and slaveholder), two other Cashaway members, two Welsh Neck members, and several who were related to members of those churches. She continues, "By the third quarter of the eighteenth century, planters were already well represented among lowcountry and middlecountry Baptist churches, whereas upcountry churches consisted primarily of yeomen" (*Unification of a Slave State: The Rise of the Planter Class in the South Carolina Backcountry, 1760–1808* [Chapel Hill: University of North Carolina Press, 1990] 66–67, 277, 301). George Lloyd Johnson makes a similar argument.

[18] Andrew Lee Feight argued in his dissertation (*The Good and the Just: Slavery and the Development of Evangelical Protestantism in the American South, 1700–1830* [PhD diss., University of Kentucky, 2001]) that Southern evangelicals made no great switch from anti-slavery to pro-slavery. His approach to the subject of slavery is similar to my argument about churches' consistent but qualified advocacy of women's subjection.

Hassell and Hassell, Old School Baptist churches on both sides of the Mason-Dixon Line remained united.

The moral economy of church discipline did change subtly over time. This study concludes at a time in which many church records reflect a shift of tone and emphasis. Discipline cases declined as baptisms and petitions for membership increased. More Southerners were joining churches; fewer were being disciplined out. This pattern appeared at the beginning of the nineteenth century in the Low Country. Up Country churches were still practicing church discipline in the 1820s, but there too membership lists were growing longer as accounts of discipline cases became fewer in number and more vague in their denunciation of offenses. As Wills has shown, discipline was still common in many churches after the Civil War. Perhaps relative isolation played a role in sheltering some Up Country churches from religious and civil networks that would have hastened their integration into the Southern world. Just how church discipline declined at different rates in various denominations and locations would make an interesting study. Simply put, though, everywhere it was in decline throughout the nineteenth century. As more and more Southerners became church members, churches moved from outsider status into the mainstream. A less divisive form of Christianity came to be America's popular religion.

Heyrman recognizes that the majority of church discipline cases involved white male defendants, and those men were the least likely to repent of their offenses. After 1800 churches still disciplined members for drinking, swearing, fighting, and gambling, but with less disagreement from the majority of Southerners. As Heyrman puts it,

> it came to pass that the world of southern evangelicals converged with that of southern masters. As Baptists and Methodists alike found common ground with worldlier men, the cultures of primal honor and evangelical Christianity

interpenetrated, and their distinctiveness, once sharply etched, began to blur.[19]

When the crude Southern man cleaned up and traded the bottle for a Bible and the Southern churchman bloodied his hands carrying a rifle into battle in defense of Southern honor, it was no longer easy to differentiate between the two. Their wives coupled the roles of Christian and Southern womanhood with less compromise. But to the Old School Baptists, friendship with the Southern world was not worth the price it exacted from their old moral economy.

The moral economy upheld by church discipline in these churches was not as narrow as keeping women "in their place." Rather, it was a much broader system of subjection that encompassed all church members, regardless of gender, color, or social status. I suspect that further research would bear out that the case of these Baptist churches closely resembles that of other evangelical groups in the South. Most Anglican and unchurched Southerners likely did not experience a dramatic decline in discipline; with a less demanding moral economy to begin with, their standards did not have as far to fall. But Methodists, Presbyterians, Lutherans, and other types of churches that once upheld a stricter moral economy in their disciplinary practices all probably experienced a similar decline in church discipline. Subjection of individuals to the authority of their churches and to God was less of a concern in the nineteenth century than it had been in the eighteenth.

In the midst of such a general transformation, it may seem strange that there was no accompanying development in the area of gender. For the most part, the traditional moral economy's subjection of women to men went unchallenged.

---

[19] Christine Heyrman, *Southern Cross: The Beginnings of the Bible Belt* (Chapel Hill: University of North Carolina Press, 1997) 215, 248–49.

Why was this so? Perhaps that aspect of the traditional moral economy was internalized to a greater extent than the rest. Southern women may have been surprisingly comfortable with and committed to their subjection to men, while Southerners were less accepting of subjection in other areas. Such appears to have been the case both within and outside evangelical churches.

Several historians have recognized that Southern women generally accepted their position of subjection. Drew Gilpin Faust, for example, has argued convincingly that Southern women resented the necessity of adapting to the disruption the Civil War brought to conventional gender roles. Faust suggested that Southern women accepted their subjection because it was a part of the same system that placed black slaves underneath them.[20] When historians rely overwhelmingly on women's class and racial self-interest to explain their gender conservatism, they leave out something crucial. Poor women, not just wealthy slaveholding women, also seemed to recognize significant benefits that accompanied their position in a traditional moral economy of subjection. Such a position cut across religious boundaries as well. The doctrine of woman's subjection was clearly rooted in religious teachings, but it claimed a following that extended beyond the confines of a particular church, or any church for that matter. Allegiance to gendered subjection may have been the least divisive aspect of the traditional moral

---

[20] See Drew Gilpin Faust, *Mothers of Invention: Women of the Slaveholding South in the American Civil War* (Chapel Hill: University of North Carolina Press, 1996); Elizabeth Fox-Genovese, *Within the Plantation Household: Black and White Women of the Old South* (Chapel Hill: University of North Carolina Press, 1988); Laura Edwards, *Gendered Strife and Confusion: The Political Culture of Reconstruction* (Chicago: University of Illinois Press, 1997); and Jane Turner Censer, *The Reconstruction of White Southern Womanhood 1865–1895* (Baton Rouge: Louisiana State University Press, 2003).

economy throughout the South. In many ways, the moral economy of church discipline that once contradicted the sentiments of many Southerners eventually accommodated the crowd. But the subjection of women was relatively constant for generations.

Southern churches did alter their moral economy of subjection over the course of the nineteenth century in order to fit in with their society, but they did so not by tightening the shackles around women but rather by relaxing the subjection of men and women alike. Accommodation came not by enforcing a double standard in church discipline but by abandoning the practice entirely. Never again would the expectations of Southern churches stand in sharp contrast to the expectations of Southern society. Churches came to be less concerned with the subjection of individual men and women, or even the subjection of a church to God. Only scattered rebels remained in defense of custom as attention shifted from families and churches to the matter of subjection to the emerging moral economy of Southern society.

WORKS CITED

Primary

North Carolina Baptist Church Records

Bear Creek Baptist Church Records (1787), Chatham County NC (North Carolina Baptist Historical Collection, Z. Smith Reynolds Library, Wake Forest University: Winston-Salem NC), 1801–1859.

Brier Creek Baptist Church Records (1783), Ronda NC (North Carolina Baptist Historical Collection, Z. Smith Reynolds Library, Wake Forest University: Winston-Salem NC), 1783–1955.

Cashie Baptist Church Records (1771), Windsor NC (North Carolina Baptist Historical Collection, Z. Smith Reynolds Library, Wake Forest University: Winston-Salem NC), 1791–1925.

Eaton's[-Dutchman's Creek] Baptist Church Records (1772), Mocksville NC (North Carolina Baptist Historical Collection, Z. Smith Reynolds Library, Wake Forest University: Winston-Salem NC), 1772–1902.

Flat River [Primitive] Baptist Church Records (1777), Person County NC (North Carolina Baptist Historical Collection, Z. Smith Reynolds Library, Wake Forest University: Winston-Salem NC), 1786–1945.

Jersey Baptist Church Records (1758), Davidson County NC (North Carolina Baptist Historical Collection, Z. Smith Reynolds Library, Wake Forest University: Winston-Salem NC), 1784–1797.

Lick Fork [Primitive] Baptist Church Records (1786), Rockingham County NC (North Carolina Baptist Historical Collection, Z. Smith Reynolds Library, Wake Forest University: Winston-Salem NC), 1786–1921.

Poplar Spring[s] Baptist Church Records (1788), Zebulon NC (North Carolina Baptist Historical Collection, Z. Smith Reynolds Library, Wake Forest University: Winston-Salem NC), 1788–1882.

Sandy Creek Baptist Church Records (1770), Louisburg NC (North Carolina Baptist Historical Collection, Z. Smith Reynolds Library, Wake Forest University: Winston-Salem NC), 1771–1845.

Sandy Run Baptist Church Records (1788), Cleveland County NC (North Carolina Baptist Historical Collection, Z. Smith Reynolds Library, Wake Forest University: Winston-Salem NC), 1782–1970.

Skewarkey [Primitive] Baptist Church Records (1787), Martin County NC (North Carolina Baptist Historical Collection, Z. Smith Reynolds Library, Wake Forest University: Winston-Salem NC), 1786–1876.

South Fork of Roaring River Baptist Church Records (1779), Wilkes County NC (original records copied by Mr. and Mrs. Stratton Hammon, Louisville KY, fmoran.com/wilkes/roaring.html), 1785–1797.

Wheeleys [Primitive] Baptist Church Records (1791), Bushy Fork NC (North Carolina Baptist Historical Collection, Z. Smith Reynolds Library, Wake Forest University: Winston-Salem NC), 1791.

Yadkin Baptist Church Records (1779), Patterson NC (North Carolina Baptist Historical Collection, Z. Smith Reynolds Library, Wake Forest University: Winston-Salem NC), 1787–1839.

South Carolina Baptist Church Records

Ashley River Baptist Church Records (1736), Charleston SC (South Carolina Baptist Historical Collection, James B. Duke Library, Furman University, Greenville SC), 1736–1769.

Black Creek Baptist Church Records (1798), Darlington SC (South Carolina Baptist Historical Collection, James B. Duke Library, Furman University, Greenville SC), 1798–1896.

Boiling Springs Baptist Church Records (1772), Spartanburg SC (South Carolina Baptist Historical Collection, James B. Duke Library, Furman University, Greenville SC), 1792–1822.

Brushy Creek Baptist Church Records (1795), Greenville SC (South Carolina Baptist Historical Collection, James B. Duke Library, Furman University, Greenville SC), 1794–1827.

Bush River Baptist Church Records (1771), Newberry SC (South Carolina Baptist Historical Collection, James B. Duke Library, Furman University, Greenville SC), 1791–1949.

Cashaway[-Mount Pleasant-Mechanicsville] Baptist Church Records (1767), Darlington SC (South Carolina Baptist Historical Collection, James B. Duke Library, Furman University, Greenville SC), 1767–1867. Cashaway and Mount Pleasant merged in 1791 and renamed the church Mechanicsville in 1818.

Cedar Spring[s] Baptist Church Records (1786), Spartanburg SC (South Carolina Baptist Historical Collection, James B. Duke Library, Furman University, Greenville SC), 1794–1972.

Clear Springs Baptist Church Records (1803), Greenville SC (South Carolina Baptist Historical Collection, James B. Duke Library, Furman University, Greenville SC), 1803–1953.

First Woodruff Baptist Church Records (1787), Spartanburg County SC (Southern Baptist Historical Library and Archives, Southern Baptist Convention, Nashville TN), 1787–1804.

Gum Branch Baptist Church Records (1796), Darlington SC (South Carolina Baptist Historical Collection, James B. Duke Library, Furman University, Greenville SC), 1796–1953.

Reedy River Baptist Church Records (1788), Greenville SC (South Carolina Baptist Historical Collection, James B. Duke Library, Furman University, Greenville SC), 1799–1914.

Shoal Creek Baptist Church Records (1795), Oconee SC (South Carolina Baptist Historical Collection, James B. Duke Library, Furman University, Greenville SC), 1796–1853.

Turkey Creek Baptist Church Records (1785), Abbeville SC (South Carolina Baptist Historical Collection, James B. Duke Library, Furman University, Greenville SC), 1785–1909.

Tyger Baptist Church Records (1793), Greenville SC (South Carolina Baptist Historical Collection, James B. Duke Library, Furman University, Greenville SC), 1801–1911.

Welsh Neck Baptist Church Records (1738), Darlington SC (South Carolina Baptist Historical Collection, James B. Duke Library, Furman University, Greenville SC), 1737–1991.

Other Church Records

Bush River Monthly Meeting, Society of Friends, Men's Minutes. Newberry County SC, 1772. South Carolina Department of Archives and History, Columbia SC.

Cane Creek Monthly Meeting, Society of Friends, Women's Minutes. Union County SC, 1789–1790. South Carolina Department of Archives and History, Columbia SC.

St. David's Parish Vestry Minutes, 1768–1785, South Carolina Department of Archives and History, Columbia SC.

Stoney Creek Independent Presbyterian Church, *Covenant and Confession*, "Of

Marriages." South Carolina Department of Archives and History, Columbia SC.

Other Primary Sources

Allestree, Richard. *The Ladies Calling*. Part 2. Section 2. "Of Wives." Oxford: At the Theater in Oxford, 1673.

Asplund, John. *The Annual Register of the Baptist Denomination in North America*. 1791. Reprint. Lafayette TN: Church History Research and Archives, 1979.

Charleston Baptist Association. *Summary of Church Discipline*. Charleston: Charleston Baptist Association, 1783.

Cowper, William. "The Mahometan Hog: A Tale." *The Gentleman's Magazine*, September 1780.

Early, John. *John Early Diary*. 1807–1814. Southern Historical Collection, Louis Round Wilson Special Collections Library, University of North Carolina, Chapel Hill NC.

Edwards, Morgan. *The Customs of Primitive Churches*, vol. 8. Philadelphia: Andrew Steuart, 1768.

Hart, Oliver. *Oliver Hart Diary*, 1741–1780. Oliver Hart Papers, South Caroliniana Library, Columbia SC.

Hart, Oliver. "Dancing Exploded, A sermon shewing the unlawfulness, sinfulness, and bad consequences of balls, assemblies, and dances in general." Charleston: David Bruce, 1778.

Henry, Matthew. *Matthew Henry's Commentary on the Whole Bible*. 1706. Reprint. Grand Rapids: Zondervan Publishing House, 1978.

Gill, John. "Of Private Worship, or of Various Duties, Domestic, Civil, and Moral." *A Complete Body of Doctrinal and Practical Divinity*. Book 4. London: W. Winterbotham, 1796.

Pattillo, Henry. *The Plain Planter's Family Assistant*. Wilmington DE: James Adams, 1787.

Rudisill, Horace Fraser. *The Diaries of Evan Pugh, 1762–1801*. Florence SC: St. David's Society, 1993.

Rush, Benjamin. *Inquiry into the effects of ardent spirits on the human body and mind*. Boston: Thomas and Andrews, 1784.

Wadsworth, Benjamin. *A Well-Ordered Family*. Boston: B. Green, 1712.

Government Records

Martin County, North Carolina Tax List, 1779. State Archives of North Carolina: Raleigh, North Carolina.

North Carolina Census, Wilkes County, 1800. State Archives of North Carolina: Raleigh, North Carolina.

North Carolina Land Grants. State Archives of North Carolina: Raleigh, North Carolina.
North Carolina Sessions Laws. 1790. State Archives of North Carolina: Raleigh, North Carolina.
North Carolina Tax Lists, Wilkes County, 1782, 1784, 1805. State Archives of North Carolina: Raleigh, North Carolina.

Statutes of North Carolina
U.S. Bureau of the Census. North Carolina and South Carolina, 1790.

South Carolina Department of Archives and History, Columbia SC
South Carolina Land Grants

Secondary

Arthur, John Preston. *Western North Carolina: A History, 1730–1913*. Raleigh: Edwards and Broughton Print Company, 1914.
Benedict, David. *A General History of the Baptist Denomination in America*. Volume 2. Boston: Lincoln & Edmands, 1813.
———. *Fifty Years Among the Baptists*. New York: Sheldon & Co., 1860.
Bonomi, Patricia. *Under the Cope of Heaven: Religion, Society, and Politics in Colonial America*. New York: Oxford University Press, 1986.
Breen, T. H. "Horses and Gentlemen: The Cultural Significance of Gambling among the Gentry of Virginia." *William and Mary Quarterly*, 3d ser., 34 (April 1977).
Brown, Kathleen. *Good Wives, Nasty Wenches and Anxious Patriarchs: Gender, Race and Power in Colonial Virginia*. Chapel Hill: University of North Carolina Press, 1996.
Bruce, Dickson Jr. *Violence and Culture in the Antebellum South*. Austin: University of Texas Press, 1979.
Buckley, Thomas. *The Great Catastrophe of My Life: Divorce in the Old Dominion*. Chapel Hill: University of North Carolina Press, 2002.
Burkitt, Lemuel and Jesse Read. *A concise history of the Kehukee Baptist Association from its original rise to the present time*. Halifax NC: A. Hodge, 1803.
Calhoon, Robert. *Evangelicals and Conservatives in the Early South, 1740–1861*. Columbia: University of South Carolina Press, 1988.
Camin, Betty and Edwin Camin. *North Carolina Bastardy Bonds*. Mt. Airy NC: B. J. and E. A. Camin, 1990.

Carr, Lois and Lorena Walsh. "The Planter's Wife: The Experience of White Women in Seventeenth-Century Maryland." *William and Mary Quarterly*, 3d. ser., 34 (1977).

Carroll, J. M. *The Trail of Blood*. Lexington KY: Ashland Avenue Baptist Church, 1931.

Cash, Wilbur. *The Mind of the South*. New York: Alfred A. Knopf, 1941.

Censer, Jane Turner. *The Reconstruction of White Southern Womanhood 1865–1895*. Baton Rouge: Louisiana State University Press, 2003.

Clarke, Erskine. *Our Southern Zion: A History of Calvinism in the South Carolina Low Country, 1690–1990*. Tuscaloosa: University Alabama Press, 1996.

Dayton, Cornelia Hughes. *Women Before the Bar: Gender, Law, and Society in Connecticut, 1639–1789*. Chapel Hill: University of North Carolina Press, 1995.

Dellapenna, Joseph. *Dispelling the Myths of Abortion History*. Durham: Carolina Academic Press, 2006.

Edwards, Laura. *Gendered Strife and Confusion: The Political Culture of Reconstruction*. Chicago: University of Illinois Press, 1997.

Eliason, Norman. *Tarheel Talk: An Historical Study of the English Language in North Carolina to 1860*. Chapel Hill: University of North Carolina Press, 1956.

Ervin, Eliza Cowan and Horace Fraser Rudisill, eds. *Darlingtoniana: A History of People, Places and Events in Darlington County, South Carolina*. Spartanburg: Reprint Company, 1997.

Faust, Drew Gilpin. *Mothers of Invention: Women of the Slaveholding South in the American Civil War*. Chapel Hill: University of North Carolina Press, 1996.

Feight, Andrew Lee. *The Good and the Just: Slavery and the Development of Evangelical Protestantism in the American South, 1700–1830*. Lexington: University of Kentucky, 2001.

Fischer, David Hackett. *Albion's Seed: Four British Folkways in America*. New York: Oxford University Press, 1989.

Flinchum, Jessica. "Reluctant Revolutionaries: The Philadelphia Baptist Association and the American Revolution." *Pennsylvania History* 74/2 (Spring 2007): 173–93.

Fox-Genovese, Elizabeth. *Within the Plantation Household: Black and White Women of the Old South*. Chapel Hill: University of North Carolina Press, 1988.

Frey, Sylvia R. *Come Shouting to Zion: African-American Protestantism in the American South and British Caribbean to 1830*. Chapel Hill: University of North Carolina Press, 1998.

Friedman, Jean. *The Enclosed Garden: Women and Community in the Evangelical South, 1830–1900*. Chapel Hill: University of North Carolina Press, 1985.

Furman, Wood. *A History of the Charleston Association of Baptist Churches in the State of South-Carolina*. Charleston: J. Hoff, 1811.

Gillette, A. D. *Minutes of the Philadelphia Baptist Association*. Philadelphia: American Baptist Publication Society, 1851.

Glover, Lorri. *All Our Relations: Blood Ties and Emotional Bonds among the Early South Carolina Gentry*. Baltimore: Johns Hopkins University Press, 2000.

Gorn, Eliott. "'Gouge and Bite, Pull Hair and Scratch': The Social Significance of Fighting in the Southern Backcountry." *American Historical Review* 90 (February 1985): 18–43.

Hassell, C. B. and S. Hassell. *History of the Church of God*. Middletown NY: Gilbert Beebe's Sons, 1886. Reprint. Ellenwood GA: Old School Hymnal Co., 1983.

Hatley, Tom. *The Dividing Paths: Cherokees and South Carolinians through the Revolutionary Era*. New York: Oxford University Press, 1995.

Heyrman, Christine. *Southern Cross: The Beginnings of the Bible Belt*. Chapel Hill: University of North Carolina Press, 1997.

Hudson, Arthur Palmer. *Songs of the Carolina Charter Colonists, 1663–1763*. Raleigh: Carolina Charter Tercentenary Commission, 1962.

Irons, Charles F. *The Origins of Proslavery Christianity: White and Black Evangelicals in Colonial and Antebellum Virginia*. Chapel Hill: University of North Carolina Press, 2008.

Isaac, Rhys. *The Transformation of Virginia, 1740–1790*. Chapel Hill: University of North Carolina Press, 1982.

———. "Evangelical Revolt: The Nature of the Baptists' Challenge to the Traditional Order in Virginia, 1765 to 1775." *William and Mary Quarterly*, 3d ser., 31 (July 1974).

Johnson, George L. *The Frontier in the Colonial South: South Carolina Backcountry, 1736–1800*. Westport CT: Greenwood Press, 1997.

Juster, Susan. *Disorderly Women: Sexual Politics and Evangelicalism in Revolutionary New England*. London: Cornell University Press, 1994.

Kamensky, Jane. *Governing the Tongue: The Politics of Speech in Early New England*. New York: Oxford University Press, 1997.

Kars, Marjoleine. *Breaking Loose Together: The Regulator Rebellion in Pre-Revolutionary North Carolina*. Chapel Hill: University of North Carolina Press, 2002.

Kay, Marvin Michael. "The North Carolina Regulation, 1766–1776: A Class Conflict." In *The American Revolution: Explorations in the History of American Radicalism*, edited by Alfred Young. DeKalb: Northern Illinois University Press, 1976.

Kierner, Cynthia. *Beyond the Household: Women's Place in the Early South, 1700–1835*. London: Cornell University Press, 1998.

Klein, Rachel. *Unification of a Slave State: The Rise of the Planter Class in the South Carolina Backcountry, 1760–1808*. Chapel Hill: University of North Carolina Press, 1990.

Komisar, Lucy. *Down and Out in the USA: A History of Social Welfare*. New York: Franklin Watts, 1973.

Lender, Mark Edward and James Kirby Martin. *Drinking in America: A History*. London: The Free Press, 1982.

Levy, Barry. *Quakers and the American Family: British Settlement in the Delaware Valley*. New York: Oxford University Press, 1988.

Lewis, Jan. *The Pursuit of Happiness: Family and Values in Jefferson's Virginia*. Cambridge: Cambridge University Press, 1983.

Lindman, Janet Moore. *A World of Baptists: Gender, Race, and Religious Community in Pennsylvania and Virginia, 1689–1825*. Minneapolis: University of Minnesota, 1994.

———. *Bodies of Belief: Baptist Community in Early America*. Philadelphia: University of Pennsylvania Press, 2011.

———. "Acting the Manly Christian: White Evangelical Masculinity in Revolutionary Virginia." *William and Mary Quarterly* 57 (April 2000).

Lyerly, Cynthia. *Methodism and the Southern Mind, 1770–1810*. New York: Oxford University Press, 1998.

Manning, Francis and W. H. Booker. *Religion and Education in Martin County 1774–1974*. Williamston NC: Enterprise Publishing Company, 1974.

Mathews, Donald. *Religion in the Old South*. Chicago: University of Chicago Press, 1977.

McCurry, Stephanie. *Masters of Small Worlds: Yeoman Households, Gender Relations, and the Political Culture of the Antebellum South Carolina Low Country*. New York: Oxford University Press, 1995.

Morgan, Edmund. *Virginians at Home: Family Life in the Eighteenth Century*. Williamsburg: Colonial Williamsburg Foundation, 1952.

Najar, Monica. *Evangelizing the South: Gender, Race, and Politics in the Early Evangelical South, 1765–1850*. Madison: University of Wisconsin, 2000.

———. *Evangelizing the South: A Social History of Church and State in Early America*. New York: Oxford University Press, 2008.

Olwell, Robert. *Masters, Slaves, and Subjects: The Culture of Power in the South Carolina Low Country, 1740–1790*. Ithaca: Cornell University Press, 1998.

O'Neall, John and John Chapman. *The Annals of Newberry County, in two parts*. Newberry SC: Aull & Houseal, 1892.

Paschal, George Washington. *History of North Carolina Baptists*. Volume 1. Raleigh NC: Edwards & Broughton Co., 1930.

Phillips, Roderick. *Putting Asunder: A History of Divorce in Western Society*. New York: Cambridge University Press, 1988.

Raboteau, Albert J. *Slave Religion: The "Invisible Institution" in the Antebellum South*. New York: Oxford University Press, 2004.

Rohrer, S. Scott. *Hope's Promise: Religion and Acculturation in the Southern Backcountry*. Tuscaloosa: University Alabama Press, 2005.

Rorabaugh, W. J. *The Alcoholic Republic, an American Tradition*. New York: Oxford University Press, 1979.

Rudisill, Horace Fraser. *Darlington County: A Pictorial History*. Norfolk VA: Donning Company, 1986.

Semple, Robert and George Beale. *A History of the Rise and Progress of the Baptists in Virginia*. Richmond VA: Pitt and Dickinson, 1894.

Scott, Anne Firor. *The Southern Lady: From Pedestal to Politics 1830–1930*. Chicago: University of Chicago Press, 1970.

Scully, Randolph Ferguson. *Religion and the Making of Nat Turner's Virginia: Baptist Community and Conflict, 1740–1840*. Charlottesville: University of Virginia Press, 2008.

Silkenat, David. *Moments of Despair: Suicide, Divorce, and Debt in Civil War Era North Carolina*. Chapel Hill: University of North Carolina Press, 2011.

Slaughter, Thomas. *The Whiskey Rebellion: Frontier Epilogue to the American Revolution*. New York: Oxford University Press, 1986.

Smith, Daniel Blake. *Inside the Great House: Planter Family Life in Eighteenth-Century Chesapeake Society*. Ithaca: Cornell University Press, 1980.

Snay, Mitchell. *Gospel of Disunion: Religion and Separatism in the Antebellum South*. New York: Cambridge University Press, 1993.

Snyder, Terri. *Brabbling Women: Disorderly Speech and the Law in Early Virginia*. London: Cornell University Press, 2003.

Sobel, Mechal. *The World They Made Together: Black and White Values in Eighteenth-Century Virginia*. Princeton: Princeton University Press, 1989.

Spangler, Jewel L. *Virginians Reborn: Anglican Monopoly, Evangelical Dissent, and the Rise of the Baptists in the Late Eighteenth Century*. Charlottesville: University of Virginia Press, 2008.

Spruill, Julia Cherry. *Women's Life and Work in the Southern Colonies*. Chapel Hill: University of North Carolina Press, 1938.

Stephan, Scott. *Redeeming the Southern Family: Evangelical Women and Domestic Devotion in the Antebellum South*. Athens: University of Georgia Press, 2011.

Struna, Nancy. "Gender and Sporting Practice in Early America, 1750–1810." *Journal of Sport History* 18/1 (Spring 1991): 10–30.

Sweet, William. "The Churches as Moral Courts of the Frontier." *Church History* 2 (1933): 3–21.

Thompson, E. P. "The Moral Economy of the English Crowd in the Eighteenth Century." In *Customs in Common: Studies in Traditional Popular Culture*. New York: New Press, 1993.

Townsend, Leah. *South Carolina Baptists, 1670–1805*. 1935. Reprint. Baltimore: Genealogical Publishing Co., 1974.

Turner, David. *Fashioning Adultery: Gender, Sex, and Civility in England, 1660–1740*. New York: Cambridge University Press, 2002.

Vamplew, Wray. *The Turf: A Social and Economic History of Horse Racing*. London: Allen Lane, 1976.

Vickery, Amanda. *The Gentleman's Daughter: Women's Lives in Georgian England*. New Haven: Yale University Press, 1998.

West, Emily. *Chains of Love: Slave Couples in Antebellum South Carolina*. Champaign: University of Illinois Press, 2004.

Wood, Betty. *The Origins of American Slavery: Freedom and Bondage in the English Colonies*. New York: Hill and Wang, 1998.

Wood, Peter H. *Black Majority: Negroes in Colonial South Carolina from 1670 through the Stono Rebellion*. New York: W. W. Norton & Company, 1996.

Wyatt-Brown, Bertram. *Honor and Violence in the Old South*. New York: Oxford University Press, 1986.

———. *Southern Honor: Ethics and Behavior in the Old South*. New York: Oxford University Press, 1982.

Wyatt-Brown, Bertram. *The Shaping of Southern Culture: Honor, Grace, and War, 1760s–1880s*. Chapel Hill: University of North Carolina Press, 2001.

Wills, Greg. *Democratic Religion: Freedom, Authority, and Church Discipline in the Baptist South, 1785–1900*. New York: Oxford University Press, 1997.

Zunshine, Lisa. *Bastards and Foundlings: Illegitimacy in Eighteenth-Century England*. Columbus: Ohio State University Press, 2005.

INDEX

Adultery 124, 140-142
Alamance, Battle of 5
Allestree, Richard 13
Arminianism 9, 50, 155
Baptist
independence/separatism 10-11, 52-53, 156
Bedgegood, Nicholas 112, 142
Benedict, David 15, 55, 77, 108, 154, 158
Biggs, Kedar 116
Burkitt, Lemuel 74, 116
Business meetings 18, 149
Calvinism 9, 50, 155
Carnality 62, 83-89, 118, 158
Charleston Baptist Association xvi, 10, 34, 66
Christmas 62
Church covenants 35-37
Church
discipline/excommunication 17-20, 149-153, 161
Church record books xi-xv
Civil War 160-163
Contention 40-42
Cook, William 5
Cowper, William 83
Dishonesty 104-107
Divorce/remarriage 125-128, 142-147
Drunkenness 58, 63-67, 75-78
Early, John 2, 62, 68
Edwards, Joshua 75
Edwards, Morgan 5, 15-16, 26
Family worship 115
Financial responsibility 98-101
Fornication 119-122, 130-132
Furman Richard 160
Gambling 60, 88, 102
Gossip 43-45
Great Awakenings 2, 9, 22, 155
Hart, Oliver 6, 63, 116
Henry, Matthew 11
Heresy 50-56
Historiography
of Church discipline 32, 149-153
of Southern manhood 60-63
of Women and religion in the South iix-x
of Women in public sphere 92
Horse racing 61, 88
Illegitimacy 120-122, 133-135
Infanticide 122-124
Kehukee Baptist Association xvi, 18-19, 29, 35, 39, 41
Landownership 66-68, 72
Lying/falsehood 47-50
Marital conflict/abuse 135-138
Membership lists 20-22
Methodism 14-15
Missions 154-156
Moral economy x, 162-164
Non-attendance 37-40
Norris, Thomas 6
Parental authority 7-8, 118
Pattillo, Henry 12
Pelot, Francis 116

Philadelphia Baptist
Association 10, 25
Pugh, Evan 6, 113
Quaker marriages 117
Regional diversity xvi, 9, 65-70
Regular/Particular Baptists 9
Regulator Movements 4, 65, 159
Revolution, American 4-6, 124
Rush, Benjamin 60
Sabbath-breaking 89, 102-104
Sandy Creek Baptist
Association 5, 9, 35
Separate Baptists 9, 15
Separation, marital 138-139
Silence of women 24-31
Skewarkey Baptist Church 69-74
Slavery
master/servant relationship 6
slave ownership among church members 68-70, 73-74
discipline cases 108-110
Welsh Neck 110-113
remarriage 143-147
sectional identity 159-160
Stephens, John 75
Subjection x, 3, 163
Suspension 18-19
Tax lists 69-72
Tithe 92-97
Violence 60, 79-83
Vulgarity 45-47, 79
Wadsworth, Benjamin 14
Welsh Neck Baptist Church
110-114
Williams, Robert 112
Winchester, Elhanan 23, 51
Wives, submission of 8, 11-17